"Jenny and Evan Owens have created a [barcode] T0059636
have carved a path to walk into healing, freedom, and ~~~
They show us how to walk the new path to healing. The 'how'
makes their work practical. Even more, they take us on a journey
back to how we are created, to the places of healing that 'medicine
won't reach and surgery can't touch.' For those individuals who
are willing, they walk with them to a healing and understanding
that inspires the recovering person to carry the message of restoration to others. This process makes *Healing What's Hidden* a
masterpiece that can tolerate the hard questions and harsh challenges that trauma brings to all of us. Far beyond the thousands
who have already been helped by the Owens's ministry, I pray that
so many more find healing in this book's pages."

Dr. Chip Dodd, author of *The Voice of the Heart*
and *The Perfect Loss*

"We all have hidden hurts that need healing but we try to manage
the pain ourselves which only makes things worse or leaves us
isolated. Trauma recovery specialists Evan and Jenny Owens enter
into your personal trauma, loss, guilt, rejection, abuse, or other
hurts to lead you step-by-step into new freedom and empowerment
to be who God made you to be. With insights from real and raw
stories, science, and Scripture, along with practical guidance, this
is a great book for personal healing and helping a friend."

Drs. Bill and Kristi Gaultiere, psychotherapists
and authors of *Journey of the Soul*

"*Healing What's Hidden* is one of the most timely and relevant
reads on trauma today. I wish a resource like this would have been
available sooner! If you are looking for an easy-to-read and easy to
digest book to help you navigate healing, I highly recommend and
endorse Evan and Jenny Owens' book *Healing What's Hidden*."

Adam Davis, bestselling author and professional speaker

"*Healing What's Hidden* offers practical tools to reboot and recover from trauma, neglect, abandonment, and rejection. Jesus made no distinction between healing physical and emotional illnesses. As followers of Christ, we are called to do likewise. Read it. Live it. Then give a copy to someone you love. I recommend this book without hesitation!"

Matthew Sleeth, MD, author of *Hope Always* and
executive director of Blessed Earth

Reader Testimonials

"*Healing What's Hidden* rocked me. Trauma controlled my life for so long. But not anymore."

Kim Hall

"Reading through this book made me confront some difficult things in my life. I was in trauma mode and responded accordingly. But this book helped me recover the optimism I once had and I accept the truth that I'm never too wounded to heal."

Kim Green

"One of the biggest things the book did for me was help me forgive myself, and it helped me believe what God says over the fear and Satan's lies."

Phil Pace

Healing
What's
Hidden

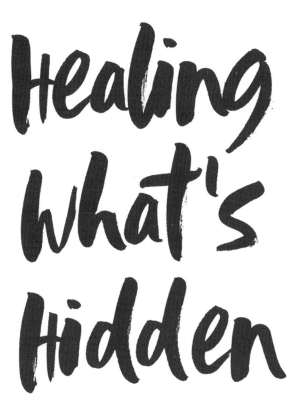

Healing what's Hidden

PRACTICAL STEPS TO OVERCOMING TRAUMA

EVAN AND **JENNY OWENS**

Revell

a division of Baker Publishing Group
Grand Rapids, Michigan

Published by Revell
a division of Baker Publishing Group
PO Box 6287, Grand Rapids, MI 49516-6287
www.revellbooks.com

Printed in the United States of America

Library of Congress Cataloging-in-Publication Data
Names: Owens, Evan (Co-founder of REBOOT Recovery), author. | Owens, Jenny, author.
Title: Healing what's hidden : practical steps to overcoming trauma / Evan and Jenny Owens.
Description: Grand Rapids, MI : Revell, a division of Baker Publishing Group, [2022]
Identifiers: LCCN 2021059594 | ISBN 9780800740948 (paperback) | ISBN 9780800742393 (casebound) | ISBN 9781493438952 (ebook)
Subjects: LCSH: Suffering—Religious aspects—Christianity. | Pain—Religious aspects—Christianity. | Psychic trauma—Religious Aspects—Christianity. | Healing—Religious aspects—Christianity.
Classification: LCC BT732.7 .O94 2022 | DDC 248.8/6—dc23/eng/20220127
LC record available at https://lccn.loc.gov/2021059594

Baker Publishing Group publications use paper produced from sustainable forestry practices and post-consumer waste whenever possible.

22   23   24   25   26   27   28   7   6   5   4   3   2

To Noah, Asa, and Judah,
thank you for sharing your parents with
hurting people around the world. The sprint is over,
now it's time to watch God do what only he can do.

Contents

Contents

Acknowledgments

To our parents, thank you for giving us healthy roots so that we could help others. We couldn't do this work if it weren't for the safety, stability, and support you provided us growing up.

To the REBOOT staff, volunteers, and donors, thank you for catching the vision of REBOOT and for going along on this crazy wonderful mission with us.

To the Revell team, thank you for believing in us and bringing this project to life.

To our friends who are featured in this book, thank you for entrusting us with your stories. Your courage keeps us moving forward.

PART 1

Your First Steps

Restoring What Seems Broken beyond Repair

You Aren't Broken; You're Wounded

Trauma brought you here—to this moment, right now.

Down the road, you'll remember this exact moment because you'll look back and realize that this was the moment things started to change. This was the moment when you made a choice, a conscious decision, to move forward in spite of the pain, tragedy, and trauma you've walked through. There are over 220 million people living in the United States who have had a traumatic experience,[1] and many of them will never truly heal.

But you will.

You will overcome trauma and embrace a brighter future because you are taking action. You are doing something about your trauma when many people do nothing.

In 2012, Jenny and I were sitting in a Chick-fil-A with our friend Jeff. He had served in the army as a medic during Operation Enduring Freedom, which you may know as the war in Afghanistan.

He was in his early twenties but had the life experience of someone much older. It took more than a year of building trust with Jeff for him to finally open up about his traumatic experiences, and he chose to do it at 9:45 p.m. in a booth at Chick-fil-A.

"There was so much blood on my boots," he began. "I remember how cold my feet were because they were wet with their blood. To this very day, I wake up from nightmares and my feet are freezing."

He paused, trying to sort out the order of his experiences as a thousand memories flooded his brain. "Why does it always have to be the neck? It seems like every time, it was a neck wound." His eyes flooded with tears as he wiped his cheek with a rough paper napkin.

"No matter how hard I tried, I could never seem to save the ones with the neck wounds. There was always just so much blood, and I couldn't get it to stop. . . . They died—they died in my arms, y'all." We nodded as if we understood. He continued, "I didn't—you know—I don't know what to do with it. I'm angry. Angry at myself for not being more capable, angry at them for dying, angry at the enemy for taking that cheap shot, angry at God for abandoning us." His tone shifted from sorrow to resentment.

"The whole thing is just the worst . . . completely FUBAR," he said as he looked away, took a deep breath, and regained his composure.

The conversation went on into the middle of the night. We asked him questions about his deployment, and he shared stories of those he had lost. He cried, we cried, we hugged, and a bond formed that has never been (and will never be) broken.

He was right. The whole thing was awful. Absolutely gut-wrenching. But it wasn't FUBAR. In the military, the term *FUBAR* is an abbreviated way of saying that something is broken beyond all repair. His story and experiences are tragic and will require years of healing, but Jeff isn't broken beyond repair.

Trauma doesn't discriminate. White, Black, military, civilian, gay, straight, rich, poor, Christian, Muslim, atheist—not one of us is outside the reach of trauma. It can touch our lives at any age, stage, or place. It can come through the actions of a stranger or through the touch of a trusted family member. It may strike suddenly as a single defining moment or seep in slowly, almost undetected, over many years of abuse or neglect. Trauma impacts the whole of us—our minds, bodies, souls, and spirits. In an all-out attack, trauma targets our self-esteem, trust in humanity, emotional well-being, and even our hope for the future. It is as elusive and tough to defeat as any enemy could be.

Time alone won't heal trauma. Faith alone won't fix it. Medicine alone won't mend it. And living life alone will only make it worse.

But you aren't broken beyond all repair.

Trauma didn't break you. You aren't broken; you're wounded. And wounds can heal if proper measures are taken.

Scan the QR code, sign up for "MyREBOOT," and get instant access to important content throughout the book.

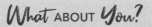

What ABOUT *You?*

In what ways does your life feel broken right now?

It's OK If You're Skeptical

Jeff was one of the first trauma survivors we met, but he wouldn't be the last. Our story began with the military, but since that time we've worked with thousands of people from all backgrounds and walks of life who've experienced trauma. But in order to show you why you should trust us, we need to start at the beginning of our story.

I (Jenny) didn't know much about PTSD growing up. I'm ashamed to say that I used it as a punch line more than anything. I had a friend in middle school whose dad had served in Vietnam. My friend would joke about how sometimes his dad would hear a car backfire and dive under the table in the middle of dinner. I laughed. I'm sorry that I didn't have more compassion for my friend, who was likely using humor to cope with what must have been a pretty challenging home life, or for his dad, who never truly came home from war. I didn't understand how fighting for your life and watching your friends die could change you in ways you couldn't explain.

But when I was a freshman in college and terrorists crashed a couple of commercial airplanes into two buildings, killing thousands of men, women, and children, the notion of trauma and its many ripple effects began making subtle waves in my mind. I found myself captivated by the stories of heroism and sacrifice—both stateside and on the battlefield—that dominated the news media.

When, in my first job out of graduate school as an occupational therapist (OT), I was told that our outpatient clinic was going to begin treating active-duty soldiers with traumatic brain injuries, my heartbeat quickened. For some reason, ever since 9/11 I had felt drawn to our nation's combat wounded. This job was literally a dream come true.

I immersed myself in military culture as best I could. I printed out the army rank structure and discreetly googled every acronym I heard. As soldiers returned from deployment, people began using the term *walking wounded*, and I knew exactly what it meant. My patients were physically fit and apparently healthy. But their legs bounced continuously under the treatment table. They never sat with their backs to the door. Their eyes were dark and shadowed, and while they worked hard to keep it together, sometimes these strong soldiers cried.

Their inner pain was seeping out of them, and I couldn't ignore it.

When an OT job became available at Fort Campbell (an army post about forty-five minutes northwest of Nashville), I felt the unmistakable tug of what I now believe is my calling. I couldn't stop thinking about it. I talked about it nonstop with Evan. I prayed. I asked God for a sign and minutes later pulled up behind a car with a bumper sticker that read Go Army. I felt a nervous excitement growing within me. Could we really uproot our lives in pursuit of this crazy dream? I was a new clinician with zero actual military experience applying for a job in which I would be helping soldiers return to duty after a traumatic brain injury. You know, driving Humvees, firing M-16s, applying tourniquets, navigating with maps and compasses, and so on—all the things a twenty-five-year-old civilian suburbanite female knows how to do, right?

But I learned, and not for the last time, that God often uses the extras to play leading roles on his stage.

Evan and I moved to Pleasant View, Tennessee, a small town halfway between Fort Campbell and Nashville. He kept his job at a web-development company, and I started working at the Warrior Resiliency and Recovery Center on post.

Here are some things I quickly learned from my soldiers:

You don't walk on the grass.

You don't show up late.

You don't tell the shrinks that you're having mental problems.

The first two could get you dressed down in public. The last could get you kicked out of the military. The PTSD stigma was alive and well.

But I wasn't a shrink.

And for reasons outside my control or understanding, my soldiers began opening up to me. One sergeant asked, "Is it possible for my soul to die? I know I had one once, but now, when I look inward, all I see is a dark, black hole." Another spoke of the crushing guilt he felt: "I stepped on the pressure plate. Why am I alive and he's dead? How do I look at his family, knowing I'm responsible?" Another described to me what it felt like to watch the life ebb out of the eyes of a dying Iraqi child as he tried to rescue him from the wreckage caused by a roadside bomb.

My heart is heavy just recalling the looks on their faces, silently acknowledging the invisible rucksacks of guilt and shame they carried. I remember the fog of isolation that surrounded them, severing them from anyone and everyone who couldn't understand what they'd gone through and from God, who, in their eyes, had turned his back on them.

So I spoke up. I began talking to my patients about God's nearness to the brokenhearted. About how he sets the captives free and comforts those who mourn. About the depth of Jesus's love for them and how he wants to carry their burdens and give them rest.

It was like they'd come upon a spring of fresh water in the middle of a barren desert. The flicker of hope in their eyes lit a fire in my heart to find a way to continue the conversation for those who were willing to meet at the intersection of faith and trauma and ask the hard questions together.

While this was going on, Evan found himself at a different crossroads. Every day, he heard me share stories of trauma and the struggle to overcome it while he continued at his technology job. The juxtaposition between profit-and-loss statements and life-and-death choices drew him to the realization that he wanted to be a part of something that he felt really mattered. He wholeheartedly joined me on my mission to serve and support military families who were hurting. Together we prayed for God to do something so big it was destined to fail without him.

And God moved.

We started meeting with couples, asking questions, and doing a lot of listening. The themes of guilt, grief, identity, and forgiveness resounded through every story of trauma as the soldiers and their loved ones openly shared their darkest and most painful memories. We quickly realized that while we were hearing repeats of the same struggles, the trauma survivors thought they were the only ones going through them.

And an idea was born: we would invite these soldiers and their families to our home, provide childcare and a home-cooked meal, and sit down together to engage the topics of faith and trauma head-on. We said, "You don't have to be a Christian. You don't have to agree with us. We just want to love on you and give you a safe space to be real and raw." It was a "come as you are even if you wear a hat and sunglasses and sit in the corner with your arms crossed the whole time" kind of vibe. And that's exactly what some of our soldiers did.

But somehow, it worked.

Evan put together a rough outline, and when he opened his mouth, it was the kind of teaching that made the hair on your arms stand up. It was as if he had read these guys' mail. It had to be God at work. How else would a (these are his words, not mine!) "chubby civilian who worked in technology" ever capture the attention of these war-hardened soldiers?

Remember what I said about God using those least likely to do his work?

God doesn't call the qualified. He qualifies the called.

What we started in our living room quickly began to grow. We called it REBOOT Recovery.

In the next few years, we saw miraculous healing as well as miraculous provision. Our group began meeting at Fort Campbell, and we had so many attendees we ran out of tables and chairs. We were contacted by people in other states, asking how they could start courses like ours. Evan left his job and began working for REBOOT full-time. We received a grant and were approached by John Dale, a retired combat veteran and operations ninja, who raised money to cover his own first year's salary. With John's help, we were able to manualize the curriculum Evan had developed over years of teaching, and we began equipping others to lead our course all across the country.

Soon, we saw that first responders were struggling with job-related stress and trauma in much the same way as combat veterans. So our team developed a course just for them. And finally, in the midst of a global pandemic, we felt the call to make what we've learned available to anyone and everyone who's experienced the upending effects of trauma. We called the course Trauma RE-BOOT, and locations quickly spread across the country.

For the past decade of our lives, we have been blessed to watch people of all walks of life overcome some of the most devastating experiences we could imagine and go on to embrace lives of joy and purpose. In this book, we are going to share a few of their stories and show you the exact steps thousands of people have taken to overcome trauma.

But this book isn't really about them. It's about you and your story and how you will overcome your trauma.

Meet Evan & Jenny and hear their recommendations for getting the most of out of this book.

What ABOUT You?

What do you hope reading this book will do for you?

Calling Trauma by Its Real Name

This book was written to help you overcome trauma. But that only works if we can agree on what we mean by the term *trauma*. Perhaps you have already wondered if this book is right for you. Maybe you're thinking, *I have experienced some painful things, but I'm not sure I'd classify them as traumatic.*

That's normal. In fact, that kind of thinking is partially what makes trauma so destructive. So let's demystify the term a bit. By its simplest definition, trauma is a deeply disturbing or distressing experience or series of experiences. If you have been abused (mentally, physically, spiritually, or sexually), been neglected, lost a loved one, survived an assault or natural disaster, or even lived in close proximity to someone who has experienced trauma—you're reading the right book.

Trauma is subjective. If you feel as if what you went through was traumatic, it probably was. However, if you feel that your experience wasn't traumatic, you may or may not be correct because trauma is tricky. It hides in the dark and trips us up when we least expect it. It plays dirty. It tries to convince us that what we experienced was normal and to minimize and excuse it while stacking itself up against someone else who "had it worse."

The first step in healing trauma is acknowledging its existence. We have to come to grips with the reality that what we experienced wasn't normal. Following are a few examples:

- It wasn't normal to suffer abuse at the hands of another.
- It wasn't normal to comb through the remains of your possessions after a fire, flood, earthquake, or tornado.
- It wasn't normal to have raised yourself and your little brother from a young age.
- It wasn't normal to have been completely isolated in your home for over a year due to a pandemic.

These are all traumatic experiences and should be labeled as such. But trauma tempts us to rebrand it. We say things like:

My mom just liked to drink a lot.

I just had to fend for myself as a kid.

It was just a really hard time.

He just roughed me up a little.

I just saw some combat overseas.

It was just a tough shift.

Does any of that sound familiar? We've probably all done some relabeling at one point or another in our lives. While doing so is very common, it isn't helpful.

When we dismiss or excuse our trauma as simply a regular part of life, we deny its impact on us. And by doing so, we risk incorrectly assigning blame to ourselves and misdiagnosing the cause of our subsequent struggles.

We end up focusing on symptoms rather than sources.

We end up looking for remedies rather than getting to the roots of the problem.

Here is a true statement: trauma will remain empowered to cause us harm as long as we deny its existence.

Even worse, the longer trauma goes unacknowledged, the more areas of your life it will reach. Like mold in a damp basement, the impact of trauma will spread until you identify its source. Trauma needs to be acknowledged and condemned.

But so often, we end up condemning ourselves. We're ridden with guilt, shame, regret, and despair. We punish ourselves for not moving on and getting over it more quickly. We assume we're the problem and that someone else would have handled it better.

We want you to know that what you are currently experiencing is a common reaction to an abnormal event in your life. No one expects you to handle it any better than you are, except for maybe yourself. There's no one-size-fits-all response to trauma that says exactly how you should be coping right now. The fact that you are reading this book puts you light-years ahead of most people!

You aren't *failing* at healing. You're *finding* healing.

And the process of finding takes time and effort. We work with people who feel like they've tried everything and nothing has worked. So they start to believe that nothing ever will.

Maybe that's where you find yourself now. Maybe you've tried therapy or read other books and still struggle every day. Maybe you're not even sure you can muster the physical and emotional energy to hope for healing anymore.

We get it. We know the drudgery of rehashing your story again and again so that your new therapist can get up to speed. Or how it feels to struggle with articulating your feelings and symptoms well enough to receive the right diagnosis. We understand what it's like to leave an appointment with another new prescription, weighing the risks and rewards, uncertain if the potential benefits are worth the side effects. Round and round it goes, each cycle a bit more frustrating and discouraging than the last.

> Trauma will remain *empowered* to cause us harm as long as we deny its *existence.*

But perhaps these attempts to heal aren't failures. Perhaps they are part of the process of finding healing. Physical healing is usually defined as the absence of discomfort or pain. But what about trauma healing? It isn't so cut-and-dried when it comes to healing emotional, mental, and spiritual wounds. What if all your "failed attempts" were actually peeling back layers to help you get to the heart of the problem?

Chances are you aren't sure exactly what to expect from the journey you've just begun in this book. You're only a few pages in, and you're wondering where all this is headed. We see this as a good thing because our destination and definition of healing may be different from what you'd expect.

There are over one thousand different therapies designed to help those who have experienced trauma, and almost all of them aim to reduce symptoms. But that isn't our primary objective for this book. While it may likely happen, it isn't our main goal. Furthermore, our goal isn't to teach you how to cope with your symptoms or to help you research new treatment options.

Our goal is to help you heal the hidden wounds of trauma so that you can embrace a brighter future. While we can't promise that your symptoms will go away, we can promise that you can live a life full of joy, purpose, and freedom in spite of them.

We believe that healing from trauma ends in empowerment—empowerment to move forward despite the past and empowerment to help others by sharing your unique story, even while it's still unfolding. That's where we're headed, that's our destination. Completing this book may be difficult, but rest assured, it will be worth it.

What ABOUT *You?*

Looking back at your life, what events might be considered traumatic? Just briefly list them for now. What, if anything, have you tried already in order to heal from those experiences? Did it work? Why or why not?

Finishing What You Start

Whether it was a trial, a tragedy, or a traumatic experience, what you've gone through has changed you. It has made your life difficult enough that you decided to pick up this book and start reading. Your challenge now will be finishing what you started.

While this book is designed to be read over a roughly sixty-day period, don't feel as if you're on the clock. Some of us need more time to process than others. We've broken each chapter down into short lessons because trauma is heavy and we want to make this process manageable for you. At the end of each lesson, we ask, "What about you?" followed by some thought-provoking questions to answer or activities to complete. If writing is helpful for you, these would make great journal prompts too. Our hope is that you'll take time to really connect what you just read in the lesson with your past and present experiences.

If you read a lesson more than once, that's completely okay. If you need to take a day off to reflect on what you've read, that's fine as well. Get some rest and then return to the task at hand. You might be able to read an entire chapter or more in one sitting—if that's the case, then keep on trucking!

We have structured the book so that it can be easily read once and referenced often. The goal is to help you, not burden you. The important thing is that you finish.

OK, now that we've made that clear, it's time for an episode of "Things I Can't Believe I'm Sharing in This Book" with your favorite host, Evan Owens. I abuse Q-tips. Well, rather, I empower Q-tips to abuse me. I have this compulsive behavior of putting Q-tips down into my ear canal. I know, I know—super gross. Not to mention, it literally says right on the box not to stick them in your ears. But, then, why do they make them just the right size?

This behavior is so compulsive that I will pick and dig until I've given myself an outer ear infection. Stop judging me. I can feel you judging me as you read this!

I've done this so many times that my doctor now orders an antibiotic ear drop for me without an in-office visit. Yes, it's happened that many times. These ear infections are quite painful, and I usually spend three or four days whining to Jenny like I have just given birth. But to make matters worse, I exacerbate my symptoms by not following the doctor's orders. Here's the path I take instead: I consult with my doctor, and she prescribes a fourteen-day regimen of antibiotic ear drops. By day seven, I think, *I'm feeling much better*, and I stop using the medication.

Yep. Brilliant, right? I bet you can guess what happens next. You guessed it! The infection comes back—usually worse than before.

Last year, I temporarily lost hearing in my right ear, and the pain spread to my jaw. I broke down and went in to have the doctor check it out. I knew something was wrong when she said "Whoa" as she peered into my ear through her otoscope. The next words out of her mouth were "looks swampy" and "we've got to get this under control."

I love my doctor. Who says "looks swampy"?

It turns out the infection was a staph infection, and I was at risk for having it spread to my brain. Uh . . . yeah. Who knew that a soft, fluffy white ball on the end of a cardboard dagger could lead to so much destruction?! She sent me down the hall to an ear, nose, and throat specialist who had a similar reaction.

Fortunately, they got it under control before it became more serious. But it took almost ten days for the pain to ease. I'd like to believe that I learned an important lesson through that experience: infections in the body must be completely eradicated, or they return stronger and more deadly. If treatment is halted too soon, the infection spreads and strengthens. Healing becomes more difficult.

Your situation is much the same. If you don't deal with the trauma now, or only partially deal with it, the effects will compound, and life will become more unmanageable. Taking half a prescription won't eliminate an ear infection any more than reading a few chapters of this book will heal your trauma.

You may be feeling overwhelmed, scared, angry, or anxious right now. But don't allow shame, guilt, or regret to be added to that list of feelings by quitting before you've allowed the healing process to run its course.

Set your intentions from the start that you will finish what you began. Nothing worth having comes easy. Anyone can start something new. It's seeing it through to completion that's the hard part. Starting things is fun. But it is the remaining 80 percent, the slow and tedious part of the process, that really matters. Yet this is the part where most people quit.

Don't quit. If you get overwhelmed, rest.

But don't quit.

What in your life could hinder your completion of the healing process laid out in this book? What could you do now to help yourself overcome these future hindrances?

Healing Won't Be like an HGTV Show

We want to set your expectations accurately: healing from trauma isn't like an HGTV house-flipping episode. These shows all follow the same formula and have a happy ending. In the HGTV world, unforeseen setbacks are solved by the next commercial break. No big deal. Everyone is still smiling at the end after what looks like only a few days of work. The predictable path these shows traverse from ruined to restored appeals to us. It gives us a sense that everything can be quickly fixed with a little hard work and some tender loving care.

But have you ever actually tried to flip a house?

If so, you know it isn't a walk in the park. There are setbacks, unforeseen problems, and missed deadlines. HGTV doesn't ever feature a house that is slowly renovated over the course of years. No one would watch that! Instead, they show quick, cosmetic repairs that cover up the deeper issues. Furthermore, most of the time they end up ripping out all the old stuff and replacing it with new.

But that isn't how human beings work. We can't simply rip out the old parts and replace them with new hardware. We have to be restored—and restoration is a more complicated, costly, and time-consuming process.

My (Evan's) parents have some incredible pieces of antique furniture in their basement. Some of them are in really good shape while others show years of wear and tear. Restoring these well-loved pieces would be quite difficult—not impossible but extremely time consuming. First, we'd have to strip the old finish from the wood. This process uses harsh chemicals that must sit on the furniture long enough to dissolve the original stain or finish. Then comes the long and tedious process of scraping, neutralizing, cleaning, sanding, cleaning again, and sanding some more. Then there's applying the first coat of stain, applying the second coat of stain, and applying wood restorer, and allowing time between each step to dry.

Whew! I'm tired just thinking about it.

If it's that difficult to restore a piece of furniture—an inanimate object made of wood—how much more complicated might it be to restore your mind, body, and soul?

Healing from trauma looks less like a quick fix and more like rebuilding parts of your life brick by brick. It is tedious and time consuming and requires hard work. You'll undoubtedly experience unforeseen setbacks and problems. That's why I want to encourage you to set your sights on pursuing progress, not perfection.

Each layer peeled back, each step taken forward, each page turned is progress toward healing. And don't be discouraged if those around you don't understand or aren't able to celebrate the progress you're making.

Most of us don't do a very good job of celebrating progress. We tend to celebrate only when things are wrapped up with a nice bow and the "episode" has a happy resolution. As a culture, we've been conditioned to respond to stories that mirror the narrative arc we've seen on TV shows, no matter how unrealistic or unachievable they may be in real life.

Communities of faith aren't immune to this attraction either. As church members, we love clear-cut redemption stories. The couple on the verge of divorce goes to a marriage retreat, experiences a breakthrough, and stands on stage a few days later to tell their story of reconciliation. Standing ovation! Or the story of a guy who goes on a men's retreat and decides to get right with the Lord—put that on a video and we open the service with it!

These are moments of celebration that are easy to understand. They fit into the story framework we've seen millions of times, and we can comprehend them without burning many mental calories. Our brains are drawn toward the simplicity of transformation.

I wish it were that simple for you. I wish that your story would fit into a flawless arc from hurt to healed. But overcoming trauma rarely fits into such an uncomplicated framework.

Instead, our stories are messy, unpredictable, and complex. They more closely resemble an epic four-thousand-page novel than a reality TV show. Our healing stories are marked by profound character development, plot twists, disappointments, and unexpected victories. When we try to force them into a prefabricated narrative structure, we discount the progress we're making and miss out on the joy of each accomplishment.

Healing from trauma probably won't bring you back to your pretraumatized self because the scars will always be there. But here's the good news: the scars will serve to remind you of what you've overcome. And someday, they will be a powerful testimony to others of what God has done in your life. There's beauty in this kind of renewal. There's a richness found in things that have been truly restored rather than cosmetically dressed up or replaced.

Imagine yourself, a year from now, sitting down with someone who has experienced a trauma similar to yours and speaking words of hope and encouragement to them—knowing that what you speak is true because you've lived it! How incredible would it feel to see purpose in your pain?

Each of us comes to this book from a different place in our healing journeys. Some of us are in the phase of having our old stains and finishes stripped from us as we work on removing the years of wear, tear, and trauma. Others of us are at the stage when we are starting to envision the end product—a future in which trauma doesn't control our every moment. Maybe we are beginning to feel like an upgraded version of our old selves.

Regardless of what stage of healing we're at right now, we are all works in progress. God knows exactly which parts are wounded and what will be required in order for them to heal. He has restored millions of wounded minds, bodies, and souls throughout history, and he is paying special attention to your wounds right now. He is preparing them for healing.

God isn't interested in HGTV fixes. His will for you is that you may experience true, lasting healing, which can come only by addressing the deeper issues.

Take it from us. All around the world God is redeeming that which seems irredeemable: "He who was seated on the throne said, 'Behold, I am making all things new'" (Rev. 21:5 ESV). Notice that God says he is making all things new, *not* that he is making all new things. God's innate reaction to brokenness is restoration—not replacement.

Just because you've been hurt doesn't mean you are damaged goods that should be set aside or discarded. You are valuable to God. You aren't disposable or replaceable. He made only one of you. He isn't going to toss you in the trash because you are wounded.

Disclaimer: spirituality is an intensely personal thing. We know that people with all sorts of feelings and beliefs about faith and religion are going to read this book. Some of you may be devout, never wavering or questioning God's goodness. Others of you may not trust God—and it's even possible you've been hurt by people claiming to act on his behalf. Perhaps even our use of spiritual language is a trigger to you due to spiritual abuse you've encountered. If that's true for you, we are so sorry.

Nearly four in ten people who don't attend church in America departed after an ugly incident that deeply hurt them.[2] Consider that for a moment. A substantial portion of the nation's non-Christian population is composed of people who at one time considered themselves to be Christian.

We've found that the main reason people have a difficult time trusting God is because they don't trust those who follow him. That's partially because as Christians we claim to be reliable, trustworthy ambassadors of God, though sometimes we're unable to live up to those intentions when the rubber hits the road.

The hard truth is that Christians don't always represent Christ. Faith and religion have been used to manipulate people or to build self-serving empires of fame, money, and power. That's not what we're doing here. The last thing we want you to think is that we are trying to trick you into agreeing with our faith perspective. If you aren't a person of Christian faith, this book is still for you. The application of the material in this book will still help you heal. If, as you read, you find yourself annoyed or frustrated that we return to Christian faith-based principles or ideologies, we hope you'll afford us some grace and recognize that we're speaking from our worldview and offering a perspective that may enrich or enlighten yours. We may come from different perspectives, but we have the same goal, and that is to help you heal.

What ABOUT You?

How would you describe the stage of healing you find yourself at right now? Just starting out? Partway through and gaining momentum? Stalled? On the verge of a breakthrough? Empowered to help someone else?

Shutting Down Destructive Responses

The Four Default Responses to Trauma

Evan isn't allowed to make home repairs. He's not even allowed to hang pictures on the walls. This is something we've both agreed upon. Some people are blessed with the "handy" gene and some aren't—and let's just say, he "aren't." Not only do our Saturday home projects typically end in a massive fight but they also usually have to be redone. A few years ago, we were trying to repair a wooden door that had been cracked due to some weather rot. Evan insisted he could fix it, but the longer he worked on it, the worse he made it. Finally, after two days of trying, we hired someone to come and re-repair the door. As the professional looked at the door, he said, "I wish you would have called me before you did all of this. Unfortunately, it's going to take more work now than if you had called me in the first place."

When it comes to trauma, many of us insist that we can fix it on our own. We want to believe that some self-care and a few good books will be enough to heal our wounds. That may work for some. But for most of us, our DIY attempts to overcome trauma will lead to frustration, discouragement, and in some cases, more woundedness.

The COVID-19 pandemic exposed the harsh reality that many of us weren't mentally, emotionally, or spiritually ready for uncertainty paired with prolonged separation from each other. Some people lived in fear, wondering how they were going to pay their bills or keep their aging parents healthy. Some were glued to social media and news coverage, watching reports pour in by the minute, tracking every detail, and wondering when it was all going to come crashing down. Others abused medications, pornography, or illegal drugs to cope with the added stress.

We all seemed to be asking the same question: What will come next?

When the virus first began to spread, our team at REBOOT Recovery met to consider how we might be able to help. We had helped thousands of people heal from trauma after it had already taken place, but could we help people while a crisis was actively unfolding? What if we could tell them what to expect mentally, emotionally, and spiritually while they faced the reality of a COVID-controlled world? In other words, if they knew what to expect, would it help them avoid the pitfalls of crisis and trauma? In truth, we weren't just doing this for others; we were doing it for ourselves as well in hopes that it would give us a guide to navigating the complex feelings we were experiencing.

We began feverishly mapping out the behavior patterns following trauma that we had observed over the years. By the end of our time together, one thing had become crystal clear: our default set of actions following a traumatic event usually makes things worse—not better.

By *default*, we are referring to those actions that people tend to take if intentional discipline isn't applied to their choices. We identified four primary default responses: first, we *deny*, then we *cry*, then we *numb*, then we *run*.

From this rough outline, we created a free online course that showed people how to recognize and respond to these dangerous default patterns. The course went viral. Thousands of people came to our website, the Department of Health and Human Services asked us to join a nationwide effort, and we even spoke about it on national news outlets.

It was truly incredible. For years, Evan and I had wished we were able to intercept trauma earlier in the lives of those we served. We often talked about how poor decisions following a traumatic event compounded the devastation it caused and how those choices often hindered and delayed healing. And now, for the first time, we were in a position to be able to prevent trauma from taking control.

You may be thinking, *Well, my trauma occurred a long time ago, so prevention would have been nice, but it's too late.*

Allow me to challenge that assumption. A big part of trauma healing is limiting exposure to *new* trauma. In other words, prevention is part of intervention. The default stages of deny, cry, numb, and run aren't unavoidable. In fact, we can learn to preempt our knee-jerk reactions and respond with alternative choices that lead to healing. But before we learn how to respond productively, we must understand how these default responses work so that we can spot them when they crop up.

Access our crisis course now.

What ABOUT You?

How has a DIY approach to healing worked / not worked for you in the past?

We Deny

The first default response to trauma is to *deny*. Humans truly do have a remarkable ability to ignore reality.

We see this everywhere, from alcoholics who swear they're just social drinkers to those who continue to spend money extravagantly even after losing their jobs. Truthfully, none of us are immune to getting stuck in denial when our lives slip into crisis.

When trauma first occurs, one of our most common reactions is denial. When our world is shaken to its core, our involuntary response is to deny that the experience will have any long-term impact on our lives. We may downplay the severity of the experience and brush it under the rug as a temporary struggle, or we may excuse the behavior of those who hurt us. This is because it's nearly impossible, at the time of crisis, for our brains to adapt to a new reality that may be vastly different from what we previously experienced or imagined of the future.

Our denial isn't driven by stupidity or ignorance; it's a natural response to unwelcome information. Denial happens when our new reality is incongruent with the way we saw our lives playing out. It occurs when our posttrauma reality becomes too complicated, confusing, painful, or chaotic to fit into our lives. We deny when we can't see how our lives can progress if we actually deal with what happened.

Feeling overwhelmed, we stuff our feelings in our emotional trash can and promise to deal with them someday in the future. We fear that if we open Pandora's box, everything will come spilling out. We procrastinate because to feel any part of it would mean feeling all of it at once—and that feels totally overwhelming. We strive to preserve reality as we wish it was or as it used to be rather than adapting to how it is now.

The problem is that maintaining this alternative reality becomes increasingly more difficult as time passes. We can stuff our painful memories away for a few months, but for years? For decades? The more time that passes, the more likely we are to encounter people and experiences that take us back to those difficult moments.

Maybe you're walking down the street and hear a noise or see someone who reminds you of your attacker, and suddenly it all comes flooding back. These kinds of triggers are common—eliciting a normal response to what was an abnormal event. The way you react to triggers has to do with how your brain dealt with the trauma when it happened. In the midst of your traumatic event, your brain stopped some of its normal functions in order to focus its effort on surviving the threat. Because of this, your brain likely didn't process the trauma completely. Like fragments of a puzzle, your memories can be jumbled and decontextualized. Then when you least expect it, a sight, sound, or smell may trigger a trauma reaction by sending a signal to your body that a threat is present. The memory fragment may come flooding back along with the emotions and physical sensations of the traumatic experience itself.

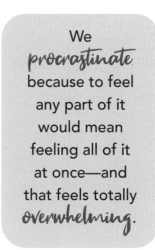

We *procrastinate* because to feel any part of it would mean feeling all of it at once—and that feels totally *overwhelming*.

In an effort to preserve an alternative reality, we avoid triggers and resort to the protective instinct of isolation. And by withdrawing, we may notice a decrease in our symptoms and memories. But just because we've contorted our lives to the point that we don't feel the weight of our trauma doesn't mean it isn't there. Gradually, we must face the *real* reality and acknowledge our trauma and the feelings that come with it, no matter how much we may want to deny them. We must bring our past trauma into the present and process it. Relabeling it, avoiding it, or denying it won't work. Either we deal with our trauma, or our trauma will deal with us.

What ABOUT You?

Does this default response resonate with you? If so, how?

We Cry

The second default response to trauma is to *cry*. As the reality of the trauma washes over us, we experience a tidal wave of complex emotions. Some of us may weep at the wreckage left in its wake. We find ourselves crying in response to a simple, "How are you doing?" We may feel complete terror at the thought or sight of those who harmed us. Others of us will feel more aggressive emotions such as anger or rage. We may find ourselves getting easily annoyed and lashing out at those closest to us. Rather than managing our emotions, they get the best of us and end up making life harder.

Despite the tight lid we put on them, like a boiling pot of water, our emotions will bubble over at inconvenient times. While standing in line at a fast-food restaurant, we may suddenly feel panic. Or while hanging out with friends, we might be overwhelmed by a sudden wave of sadness. When our emotions begin interfering with daily functioning, clinical terms like *anxiety* and *depression* start being used. We become symptomatic.

And the longer a trauma goes unaddressed, the more symptomatic we are likely to become.

Stephanie was twenty-nine years old, newly engaged, and eagerly awaiting her wedding day. She had that unmistakable glow that is found only when someone finds true love. Her fiancé, Mitch, who was a cop in town, was an all-American-type guy—the kind they base TV characters on. She said, "We were on our way to the dream, you know? We had already purchased a new home that we were going to live in together. We had paid for the wedding cake, the flowers . . . all of it." She paused to grab some tissues as if she was preparing for what was about to come. "I was about to take my lunch break when my boss walked into my office and said that one of Mitch's friends and coworkers was in the lobby and asking to speak with me."

She shifted in her chair, leaning forward and staring down at the ground as if there were a script written on the carpet for what to say next. "I assumed it was something about the bachelor party. But as soon as I rounded the corner and saw him, I knew something was wrong."

She began to cry as if she were remembering it for the first time. "Stephanie," he'd said, "I have some news about Mitch." She'd tucked her hair behind her ear, bracing herself for what would come next. "He was brought to the hospital after being involved in a traffic accident. Unfortunately, his injuries were severe and . . . he didn't . . . he didn't survive."

Over the next three weeks, Stephanie and her mom had to cancel honeymoon plans, back out of the contract on the house, cancel catering, and contact everyone who had been invited to the wedding and explain what had happened.

She didn't have time to grieve or process what had happened. She had to unplan her entire life in a matter of three weeks.

We don't know what Stephanie was like before this tragedy because we didn't meet her until she was thirty-seven years old. What we remember most about our earliest interactions is that every time we talked to her, she would start to cry. She seemed emotionally tender but not in a healthy way—more like emotionally fragile. She couldn't handle any changes to what was planned. She was single, worked fifty hours a week, and was a bit of a recluse. Her life was predictable and manageable, but it wasn't full.

It was as if her life had gotten stuck. Like a jeep trapped in wet mud, she was stuck in the sludge of her emotions. Spinning her tires, taking life one day at a time, but not really going anywhere.

Maybe that's where you find yourself today.

Maybe you are facing your trauma and are overwhelmed by the emotions that are coming with it. Or maybe the fear of falling apart has kept you from addressing it at all. We're going to give you some tips to help you manage these strong emotions in chapter 3. Feelings are a necessary part of the healing process, and stuffing them will only make things worse. We can grit our teeth and muscle through for only so long. Even if we can contain one emotion, our pain will manifest itself in another. Unresolved grief may seep out as anxiety. Guilt and shame may manifest as depression. Hurt may burst through as anger. One way or another, emotions are going to find a way out.

Against the odds, Stephanie faced the reality of her trauma and managed the feelings that came with it. It wasn't easy, but it was necessary.

The same will be said of you someday.

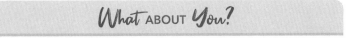

In what ways have your emotions bubbled over and impacted your daily life?

We Numb

The third default response to trauma is to *numb*. This is what happens if we don't have a productive way to release our emotions. Eventually, our innate coping mechanisms will no longer be able to hold at bay our growing emotional, mental, and spiritual unrest, so we'll look for reinforcements in the form of painkillers and other numbing agents.

Many psychologists believe that numbing is part of the fight-flight-freeze response. Driven by the sympathetic nervous system, these neurological responses are hardwired and uncontrollable— meaning they are God-given reflexes designed to keep us alive during times of great danger.

Fight is fairly self-explanatory. We see danger and we hit back. *Flight* is when we flee in order to protect ourselves.

Freeze, however, is a bit more complicated and less understood. When faced with extreme situations such as abuse, our minds and bodies may slip into a numbing mode as part of the freeze response. Most experts believe that this dissociative response is evolutionary. We see it quite commonly in the animal kingdom. The poor possum, for example, is so well known for this behavior that we refer to playing dead as "playing possum."

Let's face it, in some situations there's no realistic way we can defend ourselves. Imagine an alligator has clamped onto my neck, and I'm totally at his mercy. In this scenario, my brain will trigger a self-paralyzing response to help me stay alive. When this happens, I have neither the hormone-boosted-reaction speed or strength provided by the fight response nor the rush of biochemicals needed to escape in the flight response. The only remaining options are to freeze or die.

In these circumstances, freezing or *numbing out* enables me to disassociate from the present. To say it another way, I am physically, mentally, and emotionally immobilized from feeling the agonizing torture that's happening to me. Chemically speaking, during this time my body secretes endorphins that serve as crazy-strong pain relievers, so the pain of my injuries will be felt with far less intensity. Not to mention, if I'm not putting up a fight, the alligator might get bored and release me.

Essentially, if we can't make the threat retreat, we retreat into ourselves in order to block out what's far too terrifying or painful to process.

Does any of this sound familiar to you?

If your trauma occurred when you were a child, it is very likely that your body triggered a freeze response. After all, you were just a kid and probably couldn't fight or flee. If that's the case, you may have developed an appetite for numbing out when situations became intense. Alternatively, if your trauma occurred later in life, numbing may have developed as a coping mechanism. Many trauma sufferers aim to eliminate their physical or psychological pain by resorting to alcohol, drugs, sex, shopping, or other addictive habits. Numbing during a threat may keep you alive. Numbing after the threat has passed may kill you.

> **Numbing during a threat may keep you *alive*. Numbing after the threat has passed may *kill* you.**

Numbing works against our goal of healing. While numbing out and dissociating were probably helpful adaptive behaviors as a child, they will likely become maladaptive and harmful behaviors as an adult. Instead of actually aiding us, they will delay healing and inch us closer toward addiction.

We require more and stronger prescription medications just to make it through the day. We drift off into lifestyles of distraction, fantasy, or escapism. Books, video games, social media, workaholism, exercise—while not all bad in and of themselves—may become distractions from addressing the root of what's really going on. While these substitutes provide temporary relief, they lose their effectiveness over time. So in order to maintain numbness, we must continually find new ways to cope.

How has numbing out preserved or protected you in the past? How, if at all, might it be detrimental to your healing?

We Run

The fourth default response to trauma is to *run*. And some of us are professional runners. We run from numbing agent to numbing agent. We run from one bad relationship to another, from one party to the next. We run to spend money we don't have on things we don't need and won't have time to use. Most tragically, many of us run away from one traumatic experience right into another.

Surprisingly, staying numb requires an enormous amount of time and energy. Some of the most exhausted and overwhelmed trauma survivors we've ever encountered are numb. But what we want more than anything is relief—even if that relief is fleeting and temporary. So we run toward whatever and whoever is handing out hope.

For some of us, running and numbing have become a way of life. Rather than pursuing life itself, we pursue our next "avoidance detour." It's quite a ping-pong existence. There's a lot of moving going on, but we aren't really getting anywhere. Feel stressed? Have a few drinks. Unhappy in your marriage? Find a new lover. Work too stressful? Quit. In debt? Get more credit cards. Low self-esteem? Get even busier by volunteering more.

You can fill in your own go-to pain-killing behavior here. Maybe the list of things you've run toward could fill an entire book. And you'd probably agree that running and numbing aren't only unfulfilling; they're also exhausting! Sure, we stay busy, but are we really experiencing the deep joy of living?

> You can deny the trauma or *deal* with it. You can run from it or *stand* up to it.

The truth is if you aren't careful, you can end up running for the rest of your life. And that's no way to live. The choice is yours: you can deny the trauma or deal with it. You can run from it or stand up to it.

With each choice, either you allow your trauma to control you or you take control of your trauma.

We all want relief, but that isn't our only goal, is it? Deep down, we want to rejoin the ranks of those who are *alive*. We want to feel again, dream again, and hope again. Most of all, we want to get off the treadmill existence that says, "If I just keep moving, my past will never catch up with me."

In our experience, relief from trauma doesn't come by pursuing relief. It comes by pursuing an abundant life.

Abundant living focuses on the uncreated, incorruptible, indestructible, eternal life found in God. Before you think we're about to break out into a prosperity-gospel message, let us explain. Pursuing an abundant life isn't about claiming a promise of health or wealth. It is about finding purpose and meaning in the life God has given you. It is discovering a life worth living in the one you already have, as beaten-up and bruised as it may appear.

An abundant-life mindset recognizes that no relationship, hobby, drug, or drink will truly satisfy. It knows that, as Jesus says in John 10:10, "The *thief* comes only to steal and kill and destroy; I came so that they would have life, and have *it abundantly*" (NASB, emphasis added).

An abundant-life mindset exposes the thieves that seek to steal our joy and thwart our purpose. Figuratively speaking, thieves are painkillers that may claim to offer relief but don't deliver. They are like false teachers and charlatans. Rather than give, they manipulate and steal. Rather than build up, they destroy. They'll take your money, time, fandom, love, and energy and then sneak out the back door in the middle of the night. They offer you an anvil when you're frantically searching for a parachute. Jesus says that these con artists ultimately bring death, not life.

Rather than chasing a feeling of temporary relief, people with an abundant-life mindset focus on the endless opportunities available to them, in spite of their past trauma.

When you stop running, you slow down long enough to let yourself thaw from the freeze response and rediscover a life worth living. And let us tell you, life *is* worth living after trauma.

Possibilities are open to you, even now, while you are still suffering. Relief is available to you, even now, while you are still struggling. Your future is too valuable, too powerful, and too important for you to miss out on it by running and numbing. Abundant life awaits.

What ABOUT *You?*

How have you tried to outrun the effects of trauma in your life? How does this method of coping make you feel?

Healing Requires Humility

There is one other response to trauma that often determines a person's healing trajectory. We separate it from the others for two reasons:

1. It doesn't fit into our clever rhyme of "deny, cry, numb, and run."
2. It isn't an action as much as it is an attitude.

We're talking about pride. Pride will almost certainly delay or derail trauma healing.

In our work, we often say, "Healing requires humility." When we say humility, we don't mean thinking lowlier of yourself. We're talking about vulnerability. We mean having a willingness to open up and let others in—even if it means risking future hurt. Humility is letting our real selves out—even if it means exposing ourselves to judgment.

Pride pushes away help on the outside and locks up pain on the inside.

Depending on the context of your painful experience, your instinct may be to push back against those offering help. You might be more inclined to grit your teeth and carry the burden alone. But take it from us, you can't win the war against trauma on your own. The enemy is too strong and too clever. You are outgunned and outnumbered. The only hope you have is to let humility lead you to healing. It seems contrary to reason, but strength is found in acknowledging our weaknesses.

Paul, an early Christian leader, knew this well. He experienced all kinds of hardship and trauma. This dude was beaten, stoned, and shipwrecked, all while being on the most wanted lists of the Gentiles and the Jews at the same time! He was a tough guy. No one would challenge that. Yet he didn't boast about his strength and fortitude but rather about his weakness. In 2 Corinthians 12:9–10, he writes:

But he [God] said to me, "My grace is sufficient for you, for my power is made perfect in weakness." Therefore I will boast all the more gladly about my weaknesses, so that Christ's power may rest on me. That is why, for Christ's sake, I delight in weaknesses, in insults, in hardships, in persecutions, in difficulties. For when I am weak, then I am strong.

Despite all he had been through, Paul wasn't denying, crying, numbing, or running, and he wasn't being prideful. He understood that through surrender he would find victory. He recognized that he only stood a fighting chance if he let his guard down.

Humility invites others to help us. Pride pushes them away. Humility permits God to enter into our pain. Pride says, "I can do it alone." Humility listens to wise counsel. Pride rejects the advice of others. Humility leads to healing. Pride leads to destruction. Without vulnerability, we are all wasting our time by pretending to be stronger and healthier than we are.

The humility required to heal from trauma is a risks/rewards scenario. You have to be willing to put yourself in others' hands—to entrust them with your story—in order to build the loving relationships and community you'll need to heal. It's not easy, and it's the total opposite of what your brain may tell you to do, but you can't skip this step. Openness and vulnerability are what your heart needs in order to heal.

Remember, healing doesn't happen simply because we read a chapter, do the homework, and put in the time. Contrary to the age-old saying, time doesn't heal all wounds. In fact, wounds that aren't intentionally cared for get infected, and the infection spreads to other areas of our lives. Healing takes hard work and commitment.

If you hope to gain anything from this process, as hard as it may be, you'll need to lower your guard and approach it with an open mind. Humility is the bedrock of healing.

A final note: while healing requires humility, it takes place in community. If you're ready to take the next step, we encourage you to join one of our in-person or virtual trauma healing courses around the world. You'll encounter themes from this book and go deeper on your healing journey. You can find a group near you by visiting rebootrecovery.com/join or by scanning the QR code below.

Scan to join a group now.

What ABOUT You?

How, if at all, do you see pride as a barrier to your healing? What is one action you could take this week that would foster humility, openness, and vulnerability?

Feeling It All without Falling Apart

Denying Emotions Isn't Natural (or Helpful)

Back in 2018, I sat down with Jenny and, after a long discussion, we decided to rebrand the nonprofit. The choice was made to switch our name from REBOOT Recovery to REBOOT Alliance. I can't even recall all of the reasons now, but we went through the incredibly tedious and frustrating process of logo redesign, website refreshing, URL updating, collateral reprinting—you name it and we had it updated.

Less than a year later, I decided I wanted to change it back. The team revolted. To this day, any time I present a new idea, someone chimes in with something like "I have a better idea, why don't we rebrand the entire organization and then change it back a few months later?" I never laugh.

After some convincing, they agreed that the old brand, RE-BOOT Recovery, was better. So we went through the entire process again, essentially "rebooting" all that we had just done. During that time, I injudiciously came up with a new slogan for the organization. It was written on a whiteboard at the office for a while: "Acknowledge your stuff . . . deal with your stuff . . . but don't lose your stuff."

The slogan didn't catch on, but I don't think it was the worst idea I've had! Perhaps I should pitch another rebrand to the team?

But seriously, we must acknowledge our emotions and deal with our "stuff" without losing our grip on reality. That's what it takes to process the trauma we've experienced.

The next several chapters are going to challenge us to deal with our stuff. We're going to discuss grief, guilt, shame, regret, rejection, neglect, abandonment, abuse, forgiveness, and identity. These topics will challenge us to dig deeper into the dark recesses of our pasts and address root issues. But addressing root issues usually produces an emotional response, and most of us aren't very comfortable with feeling strong emotions.

Generally speaking, negative emotions fall under the categories of fear, anger, disgust, and sadness. Since these feelings are difficult to process and painful to experience, many trauma survivors avoid revisiting the memories of when their wounding first occurred. And if we must revisit these painful memories, most of us aren't able to clearly articulate exactly how we feel about what happened.

I routinely sit across from someone who is unable to answer what would appear to be a simple question: How did that make you feel? It isn't that they haven't thought about it (because for many of them, it is all they've thought about) but rather that they don't have the vocabulary to define it. This challenge isn't limited to trauma survivors; on the whole, most of us aren't very adept at expressing our emotions with specificity. We resort to vague descriptors and say things like "you know . . . kind of sad, I guess," hoping the person listening will fill the gap between what we're saying and what we're actually feeling. Having to hunt and peck for the right emotional descriptors is burdensome and can even delay our ability to seek help. After all, if we can't explain how we feel, how can we expect someone else to do anything about it?

With this in mind, let's try to reconnect with some feelings that are designed to help us process trauma. Let's try to bring some specificity to our emotional responses. Take a look at the following list of words, and circle any that describe how you've felt as a result of your trauma.

Are the words you circled a more dialed-in characterization of the emotions you've felt? Are the words more accurate or specific than ones you may have come up with on your own? Did you circle more words in a specific category than another? If so, what do you think that might tell you?

This problem of being unable to articulate our feelings begins when we are very young. Some of us grew up in an environment

FEELING WORDS

Circle any words that describe how you've felt.

FEAR	ANGER	DISGUST	SADNESS
Afraid	Abused	Appalled	Agonized
Cowardly	Annoyed	Ashamed	Bereaved
Distressed	Betrayed	Awful	Condemned
Dreading	Bitter	Damaged	Depressed
Helpless	Defensive	Dirty	Discouraged
Horrified	Dismissed	Embarassed	Empty
Inferior	Disrespected	Nauseated	Forsaken
Insecure	Frustrated	Outraged	Fragile
Panicked	Furious	Queasy	Grieving
Powerless	Hate	Repelled	Heartbroken
Rejected	Humiliated	Self-blame	Hopeless
Stressed	Resentful	Sickened	Lonely
Trapped	Ridiculed	Violated	Pessimistic
Victimized	Vengeful	Ugly	Suicidal

where expressing emotion was discouraged. Maybe we were told that children are to be seen and not heard. Perhaps when we spoke, no one seemed to care. Or maybe we were told to just suck it up and drive on.

Think of it like this: if you're a baby with a dirty diaper, you start to cry because you are uncomfortable. In a healthy environment, someone will come and change your diaper. This helps you learn that others can help you feel better and that emotions serve a purpose. It teaches you the basic rule that emotions get people to respond. But suppose you're sitting in a dirty diaper and despite your screaming and crying, no one comes to help. They walk by you and ignore your feelings. Or they shout across the room: "Stop crying!" What impact do you think this would have on you? It instills a different rule: emotions do nothing to help bring comfort.

When we experience this kind of emotional neglect, we learn to ignore our feelings because no one seems to care anyway. We think, *What's the point of wasting my energy if these feelings are just going to be painful and ultimately won't change my circumstances?* This disconnect can take root incredibly early in life, as shown in what psychologists call the "Still Face Experiment." If you have a moment, I highly suggest you google it and watch. This experiment was developed by Dr. Ed Tronick and gives profound insight into how a parent's reactions can affect the emotional development of a baby.[1]

The experiment begins with a mother and baby sitting and interacting with each other. The mother smiles, talks, and giggles with her baby. Then the mother turns away. When she looks back at the baby, she has a still face, void of interaction or emotion. She remains this way for two minutes. At first the baby looks confused and thinks it is a game. So the baby points at something to interrupt the mother's trance—hoping she'll look at it and break her deadpan gaze. When this doesn't work, the intensity of the baby's reaction escalates. The baby pulls out its entire arsenal of tactics to get the mother's attention. Laughing, pointing, clapping, banging, shouting, and crying. The baby feels disconnected from the mother and remains in anguish until the two minutes are over. It is quite difficult to watch as the baby unravels emotionally and begins to withdraw, eventually no longer attempting to get the mother's attention. But as soon as the mother resumes normal interaction, the baby is able to quickly regulate its emotions again.

The emotional maturity and intelligence of those who raised us play a significant role in the development of our own emotional management skills. If as a child we were shown how to properly deal with emotions, there's a good chance we know how to deal with them properly as an adult. However, if our home was emotionally unhealthy, there's a good chance we've struggled at times to manage our emotions. So many of us are taught by example that feelings are useless or perhaps even dangerous. We're told, "Whatever doesn't kill you makes you stronger"—a phrase that I have found largely to be untrue in personal experience. We're taught to suck it up and stuff the feelings that come with the hurt.

But stuffing our emotions works against our goal of healing. Feeling emotions is a natural, God-given process. Denying or forcing away those emotions isn't. The belief that we stay strong by ignoring our difficult emotions is false.

What ABOUT *You?*

Choose three emotions that you circled in the feeling words exercise, and use them to complete the following sentence: "I feel _____ [insert emotion] because _____ _____. Allow yourself to attempt to put into words what you are feeling. Don't overthink it; just let the words come without judgment.

"I'm Feeeeeling"

One of my (Evan's) favorite movies is the Jim Carrey version of *How the Grinch Stole Christmas*.[2] The line I love the most is spoken by the Grinch as his frozen heart starts to thaw. Lying in a pile of snow, clutching his chest as if he is having a heart attack, and begging for his trusty dog Max to help, the Grinch cries out, "I'm feeeeeling."

Slowly, as his eyes widen and his jaw unclenches, his heart starts to thump.

The Grinch begins to feel.

What follows is a messy, snot-bubble-cry session. The years of hatred, abuse, isolation, pride, loneliness, and trauma all come flooding out. For years he had kept it all bottled up inside, and now he finds himself "leaking" as he describes the tears streaming from his eyes. As the tears flow, the sun begins to shine on his face. He feels "toasty" inside as he looks at Max with a giant smile and says, "I love ya."

The Grinch begins to heal.

When he began to *feel*, he could finally begin to heal. In order to feel joy, friendship, trust, and love, he first had to feel the hurt, loss, rejection, and sorrow of his past. He couldn't get the "toasties" without the tears.

None of us like the feeling of "losing it." We like control and emotions are, well, uncontrollable. Without any deliberate effort on our part, our brains assess our environment and determine if an emotion should be activated to either alert or protect us. Emotions are triggered without our permission. A rush of strong emotions can feel eerily similar to losing control, and losing control is one of my greatest fears. I have an unspoken dread of being uncovered by my emotions, a disturbing sense that if I lose control and let my emotions flow freely, I may never grab hold of my composure again. I feel as if I'll be undone. Like Humpty Dumpty, I'll break into pieces and even the king's men won't be able to put me back together.

But here's some good news: we aren't Humpty Dumpty, and we aren't as fragile as we may think. No one ever cried themselves to death. Even if it feels like you might, the math doesn't add up. Trust me, I've run the numbers. I'll save you the details, but to cry to death you'd have to cry out 6.5 liters at 2.2 microliters per minute for 5.6 years.[3] Essentially, you'd have to watch *The Notebook* about 23,900 times in a row. See? Your emotions won't kill you. Don't you feel better now?

The truth is that feeling your emotions won't kill you, but ignoring them may. Studies have shown that suppressing emotions is associated with higher rates of heart disease, autoimmune disorders, IBS, diabetes, depression, anxiety, and aggression.[4] Burying your feelings can literally make you sick.

Perhaps it already has.

So hear me plainly: the feelings that come with dealing with your trauma aren't easy, but they can be productive.

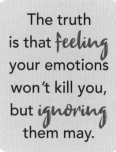

The truth is that *feeling* your emotions won't kill you, but *ignoring* them may.

John 12:24 says, "Very truly I tell you, unless a kernel of wheat falls to the ground and dies, it remains only a single seed. But if it dies, it produces many seeds." There is life inside the grain of wheat. However, there is a very powerful shell that covers the outside of the grain. This shell must be broken in order for the seed to grow and multiply. As long as the shell remains unbroken, the grain cannot grow.

From the moment your trauma occurred, you may have felt the need to put up a protective shell, to keep the world and everyone in it at a safe distance. But what if God is using this book to dismantle your outer shell? What if he's calling you to go through the painful process of breaking so that something new can begin to grow in your life?

We aren't that different from the Grinch. He was an orphan who didn't quite fit in with everyone else. He was mocked, misunderstood, and seemingly doomed to a life of reclusiveness. Over time, his complex blend of emotions was reduced to a pungent stink, stank, stunk of resentment and anger. But as he lay on the snow-covered peak of Mount Crumpet that fateful day, he reopened his heart and let the emotions do what they were designed to do.

You can't heal what you can't feel.

It took years for the Grinch to let his hardened shell break, but when it did, he finally saw the sunrise. Many of us are impeding the breaking process by refusing to feel the emotions that accompany it. Or we may be experiencing the breaking, but we don't believe God's hand is at work within it, and so we are going through the pain but missing out on some of the gain. There's a better way.

What ABOUT You?

How have the circumstances of your life begun to break your outer shell? What signs of life have you observed as a result of this breaking?

Emotions Are a Gauge, Not a Guide

Often when I (Evan) meet with people, I'll ask this question: "Are you managing your emotions, or are your emotions managing you?" Notice that I ask about management, not control. Emotions may be uncontrollable, but they don't have to be unmanageable.

God designed our emotions to be a gauge, not a guide, for our lives. They were designed to report to us, not dictate to us.

I like to compare emotions to the check-engine light in a car. Now, if you're like me, that little light doesn't bother you much. Jenny, on the other hand, tends to pay better attention to things like warning lights, speed limit signs, and fire alarms—you know, those little things. Most of the time, I just ignore them and keep right on rolling. I've been known to drive a car for months—even years—with

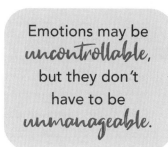

Emotions may be *uncontrollable,* but they don't have to be *unmanageable.*

that orange light on my dash. I love how every person who gets in my car tells me that my check-engine light is on as if I hadn't noticed. But what really grinds my gears (get it?) is that they suddenly become a passenger-seat mechanic, offering their opinion on what could be wrong.

"Sounds like the alternator."

"Have you checked your serpentine belt?"

I don't even know where my serpentine belt is! Here's my thing: if I don't smell, see, or hear anything unusual, I assume things are just fine. But as much as I hate to admit it, there is a tiny voice in my head telling me that there is something going on under the hood that needs my attention. I try to ignore that voice because I've got things to do and don't want to deal with the hassle of taking my car in for a diagnostic test. I mean, why can't they just have a little description box beside the light that tells you exactly what's wrong? Why do I have to take my car somewhere to have it plugged in to find out?

So I continue driving around in ignorant bliss until I actually smell, see, or hear something unusual, and by that point it's usually too late. The damage is done.

Emotions are like the check-engine light. They don't tell us exactly what's wrong, but they do alert us that something is going on under the hood that needs our attention. We can choose to ignore the light, like I usually do, or we can take our car in for a diagnostic test to find out what the light means. We can keep driving and ignore the light, but eventually we'll end up broken down on the side of the road, facing an expensive and time-consuming repair! (Not that I'm speaking from experience or anything.) When we take our car in, the mechanic comes back and explains what the light means. I have never been told by the mechanic, "The car's in great shape; you just had a faulty check-engine light." The check-engine light isn't the problem; it points to what is.

Similarly, emotions aren't the problem; they point to what's going on under the surface that needs our attention. They alert us that we've been hurt or offended. They point us toward grief after loss. In these ways, and a million more, emotions are our friends and need our care and attention. When we slow down and tune into our emotions, we give our brains and the Holy Spirit a chance to run a "diagnostic" on our lives and identify the issues that are triggering them.

But this is where many of us go wrong. Rather than recognize our emotions as something to be inspected and examined further, we let them dictate our behavior. Emotions become a guide instead of a gauge in our lives. Certainly, God gave us emotions, but we must remember that our emotions are hardwired into our fallen nature. By this I mean that sin and Satan have access to our emotional command centers and will take advantage of that access to drive us toward foolish actions. Emotions are fertile ground for temptation and sin because they are vulnerable to manipulation and misinterpretation. Emotions alone would have us follow what feels right rather than what is actually best. Perhaps the most common temptation is to link our emotions to imperatives—if you feel this, you must do that:

> If you feel betrayed, hurt them back.
> If you feel lonely, hook up with someone.
> If you feel unhappy, do whatever makes you feel good.
> If you feel worthless, end your life.

These are obviously oversimplified examples, but the point is that our emotion-based responses become a serious problem if not filtered through logic and wisdom. When I allow my emotions to become a guide rather than a gauge, I consistently make things worse. I overreact, worry unnecessarily, hurt those around me, and say things I wish I could take back.

And I know I'm not the only one. Over the years I've seen people blindly follow their emotions only to end up in deep trouble. They've found themselves full of regret after acting out of anger, sadness, or loneliness. They've hurt themselves and those around them. They've sabotaged their own success by acting out of self-doubt and fear. In a few cases, they've been tormented to the point of suicidal ideations or attempts. I've sat in a hospital room with a husband and father who barely survived a suicide attempt, and when asked by his wife why he tried to take his life, he began almost every sentence with the words "I just felt like . . ."

It's bad advice to simply "follow your heart."

Just as we would never use the check-engine light as a GPS, we should never blindly follow our emotions. Emotions operate at their best when we let them draw our attention to their source. I like to call it "looking for the thing behind the thing." Emotions aren't the thing that we need to deal with as much as they are a tool used to expose and deal with the actual thing behind them. As we feel emotions, we interpret and allow them to point us toward the wound they're rooted in.

But therein lies the challenge of interpretation. How can our emotions be filtered, deciphered, and more fully understood? And how can we ensure that our responses to these emotions are productive rather than destructive? After all, we weren't given an emotional decoder ring at birth that helps us solve these intricate emotional puzzles. We have to figure it out as we go and make the best decisions with the information we have. And let me be clear, there's not only one right way to respond to emotions but there are definitely wrong ways.

Ignoring them is a wrong way. Stuffing them is a wrong way. Numbing them is a wrong way. Acting on them unwisely is a wrong way.

But determining the right way to respond isn't always so obvious. Despite years of writing and speaking about emotional management, I find myself struggling to make decisions that are informed by but not led by my emotions. This is hard for me. That's why I have developed a very simple set of emotional-response rules. The following rules serve as a basic diagnostic for my emotional check-engine light and give me time to gather my thoughts before I respond:

1. *Emotions should never lead me to make a choice that is contradictory to God's Word.* I don't just "follow my heart." I check to confirm that I'm reacting in a way that aligns with the truth.

2. *How will I feel about this action tomorrow?* The immediate feelings of gratification may not be worth the long-term feelings of regret. If I know I'll feel differently about it on Sunday morning than I do on Saturday night, I don't do it.

3. *What am I really feeling?* I might think I'm feeling anger when I'm actually feeling hurt. I might feel sad, but the

masked emotion is really rejection. I look for the feeling behind the feeling.

4. *What is the source of this emotion, and what is the most productive response right now?* Once I've brought specificity to the emotion, I ask God to show me why I am feeling the way I am and what the best response would be. I'd like to say I do this often, but it is hard to slow down and truly listen, isn't it?

I know that these rules aren't complicated or clever, but they work for me, and I hope they work for you too. But even on my best days, these rules are insufficient unless I involve others in the process. While my emotional-response rules help, I still make an effort to talk to emotionally intelligent friends about how I'm feeling because they'll see things that I don't.

What ABOUT *You?*

Think of a time when you allowed your emotions to guide you into doing something you regretted. Looking back, what was the underlying issue and what might have been a more productive response? In the future, how can you view your emotions as a gauge rather than a guide?

There Are No Bad Emotions

Notice that in the previous lesson, I specified "emotionally intelligent" friends. That's because most people we encounter won't know how to handle our emotions. They aren't trying to be mean or insensitive; they're just poorly equipped.

They say things like "This too shall pass" or, even worse, "I know exactly how you feel." Perhaps you've tried to share your pain with someone and they advised you to simply "focus on the positive." Responses like these aren't helpful. Honestly, I believe that some people are afraid of being around anyone who expresses negative emotions. It's as if they believe that your sad feelings will infect and kill their positive feelings. Essentially, they're saying, "Don't spread your negativity over here!"

But sad emotions are not the same as negativity.

Sad emotions are like grease that enables the gears of healing to turn. They allow progress to be made in spite of the years of rust that has built up. Negativity, on the other hand, says, "This old machine hasn't run for years, and there's no chance it can ever work again." Don't let negativity have the last word.

Actively engaging sad or negative emotions won't feel good, but as the rust falls off those gears and you start to feel again, you'll benefit from the wide range of emotions that follow. Without sadness, we would not know joy. Without fear, we would not know peace.

Your feelings may actually facilitate your healing. In an ocean of sorrow, those waves of emotion may be bringing you closer to the safety and stability found on the shore. Just as we must acknowledge and deal with the pain caused by trauma, we must acknowledge and deal with the emotions that accompany it. Here's the absolute truth: all emotions are *good* emotions because they were created by God.

Let's stop shaming ourselves when we feel negative emotions. Jesus himself felt these same emotions that you and I feel:

- He felt exhaustion from the demands of his ministry (Matt. 14:13; Mark 6:31).
- He became angry at the hypocrisy of religious people (Matt. 23:33).
- He felt disgust at greed and oppression of the poor (John 2:13–17).
- He felt sorrow at the damage caused by sin and death (John 11:33–35).
- He experienced great anxiety at his impending crucifixion (Luke 22:42–44).

In each situation, Jesus allowed his feelings to bring about healing, restoration, correction, or encouragement. We can do the same because it's what we do with our emotions—not the emotions themselves—that produce good or bad outcomes. Just as anger can lead to all sorts of trouble, it can also help us fight against injustice. In the same way, our responses to worry, fear, embarrassment, or any other emotion can lead to destructive or constructive outcomes.

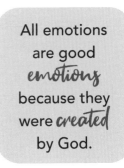

All emotions are good *emotions* because they were *created* by God.

If you're thinking *I just can't control how I feel*, you'd be correct. But even though we can't control our emotions, we can manage our responses to those emotions. We can learn techniques that empower us to manage our feelings in ways that bring about productive outcomes.

You can find a collection of techniques and strategies to guide you through your emotions in MyREBOOT. Jenny and I have included proven techniques to help manage anxiety, depression, anger, and many more. It will likely be helpful for you to refer to these strategies in future chapters as our topics may evoke some previously unexpressed emotional responses.

Access proven techniques that enable you to feel it all without falling apart.

What ABOUT *You?*

How have you seen negative emotions have positive outcomes in your life or in someone else's life?

God Can Handle Our Strong Emotions

Sure, our feelings are our friends, but even our best friends lie to us sometimes. Remember that our feelings are hardwired into our fallen nature and can be extremely misleading:

- You may feel like no one cares about you. That's a lie.
- You may feel like God has abandoned you. He hasn't.
- You may feel like you aren't going to make it through this trial. You will.

We don't have to be led around by feelings when we are led by facts. And here are some facts:

1. *God can handle our strong emotions.* Feeling strong emotions isn't indicative of a lack of faith or trust in God. Recall that Jesus felt strong emotions, and no one would doubt his faith or trust! God can take it when we feel desperate, furious, terrified, or overwhelmed. He wants us to bring the emotions to him and to let his Holy Spirit point us to the source of the emotions so that they can be healed (Phil. 4:6–7; 1 Pet. 5:5b–7).

2. *Emotions become more stable as we mature.* A newly planted tree bends and sways in even the slightest breeze. But as a tree grows, it becomes less affected by the elements. It becomes more stable. The same is true with our emotions and our faith. Reengaging our feelings for the first time in a while can leave us feeling vulnerable—like a tender sapling about to be completely uprooted. However, as we grow and survive the storms of life, our resiliency and stability grow right along with us. As we continue feeling and healing, our confidence that we can feel without falling apart increases. Perhaps you've already experienced this. Perhaps after the trauma occurred, you were

overwhelmed by emotions and unable to articulate much of anything. But now, it may be getting a bit easier to reflect on what happened. If it's not easier yet, that's OK. We promise it will be soon enough.

3. *Emotions are not indicative of the presence of God in our situation.* Sometimes when we're happy, we say that we feel God's presence. Other times, we feel his presence when we weep. But our lives consist of more than just mountaintops and valleys. And we can be sure of God's presence even when we can't *feel* him.

That's because God's presence isn't a feeling; it's a fact. Whether or not you feel close to God right now, he's close to you. He longs for you to experience his uninterrupted presence. Jesus spoke of this gift to his followers on the eve of his death:

> But the Advocate [Counselor], the Holy Spirit, whom the Father will send in my name, will teach you all things and will remind you of everything I have said to you. Peace I leave with you; my peace I give you. I do not give to you as the world gives. Do not let your hearts be troubled and do not be afraid. (John 14:26–27)

A counselor, a teacher, one who brings peace—doesn't this sound like someone we need when we are overwhelmed by strong emotions? It isn't about controlling our emotions; it's about authentically engaging them and allowing God to both counsel and teach us through them. Our feelings can lie to us, but God will always tell us the truth.

What ABOUT You?

What is one fact you can cling to when your emotions threaten to lead you into hopelessness?

A Messy Kitchen

Jenny and I have finally reached the stage of life when it makes sense for us to host family gatherings like Thanksgiving or Christmas. It's just too chaotic to travel with all the kids, so having everyone come to our house seems like the easier option.

I am a planner, so I like to have a clear game plan for when company arrives. I get it from my mom. I can remember being her helper for big family events. She plans better than anyone I know. There's a list for everything, which is timed and dated with details of what needs to happen when. Some people approach hosting like they are flying by the seat of their pants. I assure you, there is absolutely no pants flying in my mom's house. No ma'am!

As I grew up, I brought that same level of planning into my own home. Jenny, on the other hand, is much more laid back about these sorts of things. She is very comfortable enlisting the help of others and figuring things out as she goes. She always says that she's the Mary and I'm the Martha, which may be true, but I bet Martha was a better host! Now before I get into trouble with my wife, I want it to go on record that she is a phenomenal host and does a great job with everything she does, all the time, forever and ever. She's really good. For real.

But if you've ever cooked for a dinner party, you know how big a mess can be created in a very short time. Mixing bowls, silverware, dirty dishes, pots and pans—no surface is left uncovered. We don't have a huge collection of cookware, and I must have washed the same pot thirty-two times last Thanksgiving. While everyone was seemingly having a nice time, I was freaking out a little.

The enormity of the mess that had overtaken our kitchen pushed me to the brink of wondering, *Is this all worth it?* I mean, couldn't we just meet at a Shoney's breakfast bar and enjoy some of that pink foam Jell-O stuff? Or maybe we could order pizza. Something had to be easier than this mess. But as I sat down for the meal, surrounded by loved ones, and took that first bite, I found that the mess was worth it.

You see, a messy kitchen is a sign that a feast is coming. Emotions are the same way. You might look like a mess as you engage your feelings, but something good is coming. As you begin to move forward, surrounded by people who care deeply about you and a God who loves you, you'll find that the mess will be worth it.

Despite the messy nature of the healing process, what glimpses of future peace and joy have you experienced this week?

Understanding the True Source of Your Trauma

Can a Soul Be Wounded?

The word *trauma* is a Greek word that means "wound." We make it so complicated, but it's really as simple as that. Trauma is a wound. And these wounds result in some miserable symptoms.

Panic attacks, nightmares, rage, depression—you probably have your own list of symptoms resulting from the trauma you experienced. And there's a good chance that the desire to get rid of those symptoms may have been what led you to pick up this book in the first place. As we've mentioned before, thousands of treatments have been developed to help patients reduce symptoms, and generally speaking, temporarily removing symptoms is a relatively easy process. Through modern medications, scientists have made incredible progress in lessening or eradicating many trauma-related symptoms—even if only temporarily.

But as helpful as those medications can be to treat symptoms, there's no magic pill we can take to heal trauma's damage. That's because no one—no scientist, doctor, or counselor—understands or is able to quantify all the ways trauma wounds us.

But we do know some things for certain.

There's no doubt that trauma wounds the mind and body. Ample research has shown that regulating our emotions becomes more difficult after trauma. Trauma survivors often experience changes in serotonin, norepinephrine, dopamine, and cortisol levels, leading to anxiety, depression, and hypervigilance. There is also mounting evidence showing that trauma changes the physiological anatomy and performance of the brain. Studies have shown that trauma is associated with changes to the amygdala, hippocampus, and prefrontal cortex, which may explain fluctuations in behavior, mood, and executive function.[1] Stress and trauma have also been linked with cognitive dysfunction,[2] cardiac- and digestive-related diseases,[3, 4] and even autoimmune disorders.[5]

Most of us believe that human beings are composed of a body, a mind, and a soul. We've already established that trauma can wound the mind and body. Let's follow this logic a step further. If trauma can wound the mind, and trauma can wound the body, an important question for us to consider is, Can trauma wound the soul?

This question leads to other questions: How do you heal distrust and shame? What about loss of faith, hope, or purpose? These questions ultimately led us to start REBOOT Recovery all those years ago. We wanted to approach trauma through a different lens because we believed that these kinds of symptoms could be healed too.

Most of us tend to think of trauma as predominantly a mental health issue. That means that when we experience trauma, mental health professionals are often the first (and sometimes only) people we go to for help. But what if some of the symptoms we experience are evidence of a wounded soul rather than a wounded mind or body? What if we've been treating only a portion of the problem?

Certainly, if our wounds are of the mind, then mental health care is the best tool for the job. But exclusively using mental health tools to fix a soul health issue would be like trying to hammer a nail with a screwdriver. It might eventually work, but it wouldn't be very effective.

The spiritual component is crucial because trauma wounds us in places that medicine won't reach and surgery can't touch. Trauma wounds our souls. And these wounds need to be tended to. Depending on your preferences and spiritual beliefs, soul care can take many different forms. But ultimately, soul wounds need a soul healer. And we believe the only one who can repair a wounded soul is the original manufacturer—God himself.

> The spiritual component is *crucial* because trauma wounds us in places that medicine won't *reach* and surgery can't *touch*.

What ABOUT *You?*

How do you think trauma impacts the soul? What does soul care look like for you? What is something you can do this week to care for your soul?

The Roots of Trauma

For Christians to more fully understand the role God plays in our healing, we need to go all the way back to the beginning. We mean the actual *beginning*. If we want to understand the impact trauma has on our souls and how our souls can be healed, we need to go back to the time when the first trauma occurred.

We're talking about the moment Eve ate the apple in the garden of Eden. For our friends who don't subscribe to the Christian faith, consider how this story, even if just allegorically, speaks to the origin and generational impact of trauma.

In Genesis 3, we read that Adam and Eve, tempted by the serpent, rejected God's simple instructions and ate of the tree of the knowledge of good and evil. Suddenly, evil swept into the world and the first soul wounds were inflicted. Adam's and Eve's good lives were corrupted by sin. They experienced trauma. Imagine suddenly becoming aware of your faults, your failures, and your nudity all at the same moment! While the word *trauma* didn't exist at that time, we're confident that suddenly coming face-to-face with the essence and consequences of evil was traumatic.

Prior to the fall, Adam's and Eve's lives were marked by a firmly rooted sense of security, belonging, and purpose (Gen. 1:26, 28; 2:15). They were safe. They were provided for. No one was going to harm them. They belonged to each other, and they hung out with God. They didn't struggle with self-esteem or worry about what anyone else thought of them. As managers of the garden, they had a job to do that was completely fulfilling. They reigned over the fish, birds, and animals. Adam even got to name them. Life was good.

Security, belonging, and purpose—a life that's flourishing will be rooted in these words. Generally speaking, if you can describe your life with these three words, you're probably on a good path.

But then Adam and Eve chose to trust the serpent (and themselves) rather than God. For the first time ever, sin intersected their lives, damaging the healthy roots God had given them and changing everything.

Instead of security, they felt fear, loss, guilt, shame, and regret (Gen. 3:8–10). Instead of belonging, they felt rejection and hurt (vv. 23–24). Instead of knowing their purpose, they felt lost (vv. 16–19).

The same thing happens to us. God gave us a root system of security, belonging, and purpose. But trauma attacks our root system and leaves our souls wounded. These soul wounds will be the focus of the remainder of this book: the wound of loss (chap. 5); the wounds of guilt, shame, and regret (chap. 6); the wounds of rejection, neglect, and abandonment (chap. 7); the wounds of hurt and abuse (chap. 8); and the wounds of lost identity and purpose (chaps. 10, 11).

Merely words, this short list doesn't seem like that big of a deal. But these words are wounds that impact the roots of our lives. And roots produce fruit. Healthy roots produce characteristics such as peace, patience, and joy (Gal. 5:22–23). Unhealthy roots produce symptoms such as insecurity, anxiety, anger, addiction, fear, and suicidal thoughts.

When the roots of our souls are wounded, no amount of effort, willpower, or wishing will produce the kind of fruit we desire. In fact, investing all our energy trying to change or manage the fruit without first healing the roots will likely leave us discouraged, frustrated, and worst of all, still wounded. We're convinced that many of us never heal from trauma partially because we spend all our energy trying to remove symptoms rather than healing the root causes of the symptoms. We focus solely on the mental and physical aspect of healing and overlook the healing of our souls.

It's only natural that a tree with a damaged root system won't be a healthy tree. No matter how much water, sunlight, and care are provided, it probably won't yield much fruit. Some of us may be in a place where we are trying to force our healing. We are reading books, going to therapy, getting treatment, taking medications, and doing the magic dance of healing, and yet we still aren't experiencing the breakthrough we seek.

If that's you today, don't be discouraged. Those activities are helpful and will aid in your healing effort over time. But in your quest to remove unwanted symptoms from your life, don't neglect root care. Continue applying your energy there.

Recognizing that the fruit (our symptoms) can be tied to wounded roots is what differentiates our approach from many other approaches. Understanding the spiritual implications of trauma enables us to truly heal. When we say *truly heal*, we're not talking solely about a reduction of symptoms; we're talking about the capacity to flourish and live life as God intended.

How did your trauma impact your sense of security, belonging, and purpose?

Mistaking Outcome for Origin

Trauma catalyzes a conversation about faith.

When I (Jenny) first began working with trauma survivors in a clinical setting, I was caught off guard by how many of our conversations ended up being about spiritual matters. Most of my patients didn't consider themselves to be religious people, yet I was always struck by the depth and insight of their questions. It was as if they already understood that trauma was, in part, a spiritual wound. Almost universally, my patients wanted to know where God was in their situation. They wanted to know what happens at the intersection of faith and trauma. They asked questions like Why is this happening to me? What did I do to deserve this? Will there be justice for the person who did this to me? Why do bad things happen to good people?

When we experience trauma or tragedy, I believe it pushes us to ask the questions humankind has asked since the beginning of time. These questions are not easily answered, and we certainly won't answer them all in this book. But these are the right questions, and God is pleased when we ask them. At their core, they are about humanity's place in the world, the nature of God, justice, and the origins of good and evil. They lead us into the realm of faith because they force us to come to grips with our own limitations, to entertain the possibility that we are not really in control. When we are faced with the aftershocks of trauma, we are challenged with the same choice Adam and Eve were: either to trust God even though we may not understand or to put our trust elsewhere.

In my opinion, a book about overcoming trauma would be incomplete without addressing the origins of trauma. I'll be the first to admit that back when I began having these conversations, I didn't have a very clear understanding of the roles God and humankind play in this context. So Evan and I began poring over books, reading Scripture, listening to sermons, subscribing to podcasts, and discussing the topic on almost every car ride to and from our weekly REBOOT meetings. We figured if soul wounds require a soul healer, then we wanted to learn as much as we could about God and how he interacts with suffering. Admittedly, I still don't know as much as I'd like about the ways faith and trauma intersect, but I have locked in a few things that I now know to be true. Here's the first point: trauma isn't caused by God. It's a result of the sinful actions of humans toward one another. Whether we want to admit it, we are all traumatized by a horrible disease. It's chronic and highly contagious. It is the oldest and most pervasive sickness in the world. This sickness is a word that we don't even really like to say—*sin*.

Trauma is done to us but sin is done by us, and sin has traumatized the world.

Now before you put the book down, I want to be clear that I am *not* saying your trauma was caused by your sin. But I do want to help you understand that there is an intentionality behind many of the abuses people suffer. Bear with me for a moment. When it comes to ourselves, we tend to use substitute language for sin. We feel more comfortable saying we've made a mistake rather than saying we've sinned. However, there is a significant difference between a mistake and a sin. Don't miss this concept because it's critical to understanding the trauma you've experienced. Think of some of the moments of inhumanity, cruelty, or abuse you've witnessed or experienced throughout your life. Were those all mistakes? Probably not. Some of them were sinful choices by others that left a permanent mark on your life. Others' actions became your pain. They, not God, made the choice to hurt you. Recognizing that trauma is a result of human sin and not a cosmic punishment helps us align our souls with the truth.

This leads me to a second point: God is our ally and not our enemy. Too often we are misled to believe the exact opposite. We begin to view God as the perpetrator of our pain rather than the redeemer of it.

Christians believe that there is a spiritual being known as Satan who is the author of chaos, trauma, and destruction. The book of Genesis teaches that through Satan's deception of Adam and Eve sin entered the world, and sin has caused trauma ever since. Disaster, disease, and decay have gripped our world, and like a rerun of a show no one wants to watch, generation after generation has turned on each other through war, hatred, and greed. We steal, we lie, we oppress, and when justice comes knocking, we hide and blame God for not stopping our actions in the first place.

Essentially, we make a mess of things and then blame God. After all, if he's so good and loving, why did he let it happen?

Do you see now how trauma catalyzes a conversation about faith? When we find ourselves drowning in the maelstrom of life, we want to know who's responsible and we want justice. But the idea that there is a spiritual war going on—with our souls at the center—is hard to

> Recognizing that trauma is a result of *human* sin and not a cosmic punishment helps us *align* our souls with the *truth*.

fathom. We're often blind to the fact that we have a very real enemy who wants nothing more than to isolate us and to turn us against the only one who is truly on our side, the only one who knows the end of the story from the very beginning.

Rather than seeing God as our ally, our comforter, and our protector, we see him as an unjust, unkind, and irresponsible deity, a detached God who sees but doesn't intervene in the affairs of lowly humans. That's assuming we still even believe he exists.

In Genesis 50:20, Joseph says to his brothers (who faked Joseph's death and sold him into slavery), "You tried to harm me, but God made it turn out for the best, so that he could save all these people, as he is now doing" (CEV).

We frequently mistake outcome for origin. For example, a child is adopted out of an abusive home and ends up becoming a very successful child psychologist. People will say such things as "I guess God caused her to endure all that abuse so she could grow up and help other kids someday."

It's clear to see God's hand in the outcome of the adoption in that the child was rescued and put on a path to helping others in crisis. However, the *outcome* and the *origin* are not the same. God didn't make her birth parents abuse her. He never intended for children to be harmed by the ones who were supposed to care for them. That wasn't in his original plan. But when sin entered the world, so did suffering, poverty, addiction, and abuse. Yet even in the brokenness of the world, we see God's redeeming force!

God can take something that seems used, broken, and damaged and repurpose it for something incredible. I've seen this happen thousands of times firsthand. What if, by reading this book, you have begun the process of bringing purpose to your pain? Could there be a new purpose in your life now that is only possible because of the painful experiences you've had? God wasn't the origin of your trauma, but he is transforming the outcome of your trauma into something beautiful. Is it possible for you to believe that?

If trauma was your personal intersection with the brokenness of the world, recovery is your personal intersection with the redemptive heart of God.

What ABOUT You?

What role do you see God playing in the circumstances of your trauma?

A Soul Healer

Think back to the story of Adam and Eve in the garden of Eden. Remember the three healthy roots that were damaged by their fall into sin (security, purpose, and belonging)? Yes, trauma entered the world, but that wasn't the end of the story. Even as Adam and Eve encountered—for the first time in history—fear, rejection, loss, and shame, God offered restoration and redemption. Notice three things God did immediately after Adam and Eve's trauma:

1. *He clothed them.* Adam and Eve were naked and ashamed and hid from God. When he found them, he made clothing for them from animal skins (Gen. 3:21). Through this action, God covered their shame and insecurity. He protected their vulnerabilities. He cared for them when they were at their weakest. He gave them safety. He can do the same for you and me.

2. *He reminded them of their purpose.* Even though they were banished from the garden, and even though their work would be much harder, Adam and Eve still had jobs to do (vv. 16–19). Adam's job was to work the ground. Eve's was to help populate the earth. Despite their trauma, they still had a purpose on earth that was God-ordained. So do you and I.

3. *He set a plan into action that would reunite them (and their offspring) with him in perfect belonging through Jesus.* God foretold Jesus's triumph over sin and death on the cross, which would make it possible for all humanity to enter God's family (v. 15). No more rejection, abandonment, or abuse. Through faith, they would be sons and daughters of the king, receiving the protection, relationship, and inheritance that came with it. This promise is also for you and me.

As soon as Adam and Eve experienced trauma for the first time, God set in motion a plan to heal their soul wounds and reestablish their healthy roots. The same is true for you. He wasn't caught off guard or unprepared for the trauma you experienced. He wants to give you the security, purpose, and belonging only he can offer. God wants you to accept him as your ally, not your enemy. But you may not trust him just yet, and that's understandable. Perhaps you feel that you've trusted him in the past and he's let you down. If that's the case, I hope that today will be the start of reestablishing trust and communication between you and God.

A wounded soul needs a soul healer, and he's the only one who can get the job done.

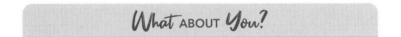

What role do you see God playing in your healing?

Symptom Whack-a-Mole

I (Evan) am often asked why I focus so heavily on the issue of soul woundedness. I suppose, for some, it can be a drag to hear me go on about all this spiritual stuff. But please know that I care for you, and I want you to find lasting healing. That's the reason I devote so many pages in this book to this issue.

Have you ever pulled a weed from the ground only to see a new weed pop up in its place soon after? Why does this happen? Because the weed is merely a visible indication of a much deeper and more extensive root system. In other words, the weed is a sign of something going on under the surface. Yes, pulling that weed will remove it from your view and restore a nice, attractive lawn for the moment, but you can be assured that without addressing the problem at the root level, the weeds will only multiply and worsen over time.

This is how it feels for many people on the road to recovery. They fix one issue only to see another one emerge. This is because if you leave the spiritual-root issue unhealed, the physical-fruit issues will continue to linger. In fact, they might get worse. What started with anxiety may turn into anger. What began as trouble sleeping may mutate into addiction.

I've seen too many people play whack-a-mole with their symptoms, chasing a cure to the point of exhaustion. As soon as they think they've identified and smashed the problem, another pops up unexpectedly in an entirely different part of their lives. I've seen people take medications that successfully remove one symptom while simultaneously creating a new one due to undesirable side effects. I've stood with them in doctors' appointments while they endured painful injections and invasive procedures designed to address the cause of the problem, but months later, the symptoms remained.

It's heartbreaking to watch, let alone experience. I don't want you to wear yourself out chasing surface-level healing. I want you to overcome trauma and embrace a brighter future. That's the goal of this book.

During the height of the wars in Iraq and Afghanistan, the army created a special unit called the Warrior Transition Battalion, or WTB. This special unit was a place where wounded soldiers were sent in order to heal from their injuries. Our first office for REBOOT was next door to the WTB barracks. The idea of the WTB looked great on paper: soldiers would be removed from their units, go to the WTB, undergo intense multidisciplinary healing programs, get better, and then return to their original placements. That's how it was planned. But it didn't go that way.

Instead, soldiers who were sent to the WTB often got worse rather than better.

It didn't make any sense. They were going to several medical appointments every day, working with case managers, and seeing some of the brightest occupational and physical therapists, speech-language pathologists, psychiatrists, and physicians on the planet. Yet despite receiving the loving care of these professionals, many of them found their symptoms escalating and spreading.

Many trauma sufferers believe the myth that they'll only get back to living once their symptoms are gone. This was the attitude within the WTB.

When soldiers left their primary units, they were told to focus solely on getting better. They left their daily job roles and often lost contact with those they had fought alongside during battle. Other duties and responsibilities were put on pause as every moment of the day was spent trying to achieve a level of function that would enable them to return to their units. Well, it turns out, they didn't live on pause very well. Their lives became stagnant, which created a breeding ground for temptation, further proliferation of symptoms, and even self-destruction. Sadly, many of those soldiers never made it back to their units. Suicides and suicide attempts climbed dramatically, addiction ran rampant, and some soldiers were discharged from the army without a plan or vision of what to do next.

I watched all of this unfold in real time from my REBOOT cubicle, and here's what that experience taught me: when symptom management becomes our primary focus, our symptoms will eventually control our lives. I learned that whatever we focus on will grow, and if our focus is only on our symptoms, they'll grow too. Over time, life will be viewed through the lens of our symptoms. What we do and don't do, where we go and don't go, our self-esteem, and even our future plans will be dictated by the presence or absence of our symptoms. Instead of controlling our symptoms, we'll find that they are controlling us.

Given enough time and attention, our symptoms will even shape our identity. This started to happen in the WTB. When I met a soldier for the first time, they would introduce themselves as "Pvt. Joe Snuffy" and then immediately tell me they were in the WTB. But they didn't do it with the same pride they might have if they said they were a Rakkasan or a Green Beret. Rather, they said it as if they were already defeated. It was their way of saying, "Hello, I'm Joe and I'm damaged goods, so I'm not much use to you or the army anymore."

In my experience, primarily chasing the removal of symptoms will lead only to disappointment since our symptoms—and the treatments we use to reduce them—are moving targets. A medication may work for a time and then lose its effectiveness, thus starting the entire quest over again.

So why do I focus so heavily on the issue of soul woundedness?

Because focusing on fruit is a gamble at best, and based on experience, I don't like the odds. But focusing on roots is a sure thing that I've seen work for thousands of people just like you.

What ABOUT *You?*

What symptoms have you experienced that might be rooted in trauma? How have they influenced your outlook and behaviors?

PART 2

Your Wounding

Loss

Living Boldly When You're Uncertain

Loss Sucks

On January 24, 1848, less than ten days before the signing of the peace treaty ending the Mexican-American War, James W. Marshall, a thirty-six-year-old carpenter, noticed some bright bits of yellow metal near a sawmill he was constructing. He didn't know it, but he'd go on to begin what became known as the Gold Rush. The population of California grew from fourteen thousand to over one hundred thousand in only a few months as men and women came from all over the country to find the treasured mineral hidden in those hills.

Sadly, most found it to be a fool's errand. By 1860, the romantic era of the Gold Rush had ended, and most of the miners left in deeper poverty than when they arrived. Even Marshall, the man who discovered the first flakes of gold, died penniless. Whether they admitted it or not, the miners' lives were ruled by the constant search for a discovery that would likely never come.

Loss puts us on a similar search. After a painful experience of loss, our minds can become singularly focused on the slight chance of finding the elusive answers to our suffering. We think, *Maybe today is the day that it will all start to make sense. Maybe today I'll understand why.* We ask, Why did she have to be the one who was killed? Why would he do that to me?

Suffering straps us with a rucksack full of questions that we lug around on our search for purpose and understanding. But the answers rarely come.

In his book, *The Combat Trauma Healing Manual*, Chris Adsit provides what I (Evan) believe is the best explanation of grief I've ever read. He says, "When we grieve, we're authentically engaging the emotions that come with loss—rather than stuffing or denying them. We're protesting the injustice of the loss and expressing that we deeply wish the loss had never occurred."[1]

I love this idea of "protesting the injustice" of the loss. To me, that's at the very center of the "why" questions. Loss seems so unfair.

We've all lost something or someone, and we can all agree—loss sucks. Maybe you lost your innocence, your hope, or your trust in humanity. Maybe you lost an ability or stood by helplessly as a dream died. Perhaps you lost a close family member or friend. Maybe, like so many others, you've cried out, "Why?" and to some degree, your life has been ruled by a constant hunt for an answer to this question. If so, I want you to know that you aren't alone and that your search for answers isn't a fool's errand.

Because it's in the search that we find a vocabulary for what we're feeling, and it's the search that ultimately leads us to God.

Loss exposes our limitations by forcing us to realize we aren't in control. Loss doesn't discriminate, and it doesn't ask for our input. It doesn't care about our feelings, and it can't be undone no matter how loudly we object. It takes what it takes, and it never settles accounts. Loss is dumped in our laps. We can't trade it in or give it away. We have to carry it.

It is as if loss booked a trip for us that we didn't plan on taking. We weren't ready to go, and we don't have an itinerary. To make matters worse, we don't know how long the trip will take or what we'll do along the way. We don't know who's coming with us or what it will cost. It isn't at all like a surprise dream vacation—it's a road trip from hell.

Most of us don't deal well with loss. We want things to go our way, to go as planned, to go as expected. So naturally, when they

How They Say the Grief Cycle Works

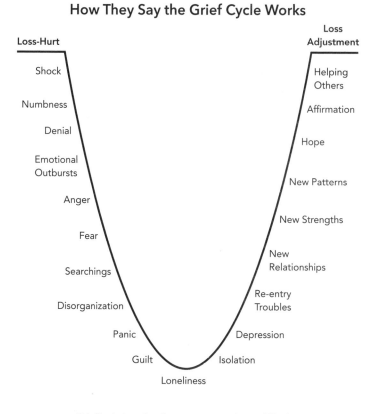

Grief is designed to force us to experience difficult emotions and process our losses.

don't, it hurts. And this hurt we feel is called *grief*. Grief happens when our picture of the future changes without our approval.

The grieving process is terribly difficult no matter the circumstances. As we protest the injustice of the loss, our grief manifests in a mixture of emotions, combining anger, fear, sadness, regret, and loneliness. There is no easy way out of grief, and there are no shortcuts. In fact, I've come to believe that, in part, that's the point of the process itself. Grief is designed to force us to experience difficult emotions and truly process our losses.

How the Grief Cycle Actually Feels

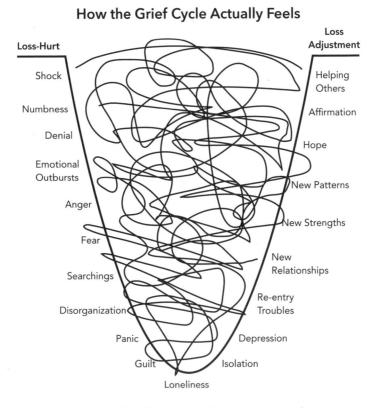

Loss-Hurt

Shock

Numbness

Denial

Emotional Outbursts

Anger

Fear

Searchings

Disorganization

Panic

Guilt

Loneliness

Loss Adjustment

Helping Others

Affirmation

Hope

New Patterns

New Strengths

New Relationships

Re-entry Troubles

Depression

Isolation

The complexity of grief, combined with our suppression of strong emotions, leads many of us to avoid processing the loss altogether.

A simple search online for the word *grief* will result in thousands of diagrams of the grieving process. They usually look something like the first image of a valley with the stages of grief neatly labeled: Shock, Denial, Fear, Loneliness, and so on.

But in my experience, grief is rarely so neat and tidy. I think the grief process looks a little bit more like the second image with chaotic jumps to and from every stage—more like a child's scribble than a logical progression. The complexity of grief, combined with our tendency to suppress strong emotions, leads many of us to avoid processing the loss altogether. In case you need it, I give you permission to grieve and for it to be a messy process.

Grief is the inner thoughts and feelings that emerge as a result of loss. Mourning is the external expression of that grief. We all feel grief, but far fewer of us mourn. Rather than embarking on the road trip from hell, we try to take a bypass around the grieving and mourning process. We deny, cry, numb, and run. But when we do that, we inadvertently also bypass the goodness found on the other side.

What ABOUT You?

What "why" questions do you have regarding your loss(es)?

People Say the Stupidest Things

The following are real comments I (Evan) have heard people make to those who are grieving:

> I hear that's the worst way to die.
>
> You've lost so many people it probably doesn't faze you anymore.
>
> At least she made it to eighty-one. She had a good, long life.
>
> God needed him more than you do.
>
> At least you're young and can have another child. Or you can adopt.

Yep, that's happened. Perhaps you've been on the receiving end of these kinds of statements. Statements like these can actually lead to roadblocks in the grieving process.

Most people don't know how to help someone who is grieving. They say the wrong things at the wrong times, linger longer than they ought, or try to offer drive-by comfort. They don't mean to be so awkward, but they don't know how to grieve well themselves, let alone help others through their pain. On some level, we all know that grief is done better with others. But the thought of facing their uncomfortable condolences is just too . . . well . . . uncomfortable.

Furthermore, people rush us. They don't know why it is taking us so long to heal and want things to go back to the way they were before the loss occurred. They might say things like "It's time to move on" or "Let go and let God." This can be extremely frustrating because we don't want to be hurried through the line to start a trip we didn't want to take in the first place! So we isolate and we hide out, hoping the pain and the less-than-helpful support will go away with time.

But let's not judge people too harshly. Their motivation to get us moving in the right direction is well-intended; it's just overshadowed by their desire to not feel bummed out when they interact with us. And to their credit, knowing how to interact appropriately with someone who is hurting is more challenging than it seems. I've even found myself caught between feeling awkward if I say something and guilty if I don't. What questions can I ask? Asking "How have you been?" is obviously wrong because I know they feel terrible, but how else do conversations get started? That's like my only go-to opening line. And what should I talk about? If I share something good going on in my life, I feel guilty for what feels like gloating in light of their suffering. Conversely, if I complain about something difficult in my life, I appear ungrateful or oblivious to the depth of pain they've experienced.

There's an internal monologue that plays in my head before I go into a coffee shop to meet with someone who is struggling. I remind myself of how sensitive the situation is and how I better pick my words extremely carefully. It causes serious conversation anxiety. I even catch myself rehearsing the questions and stories I'll share during our interaction to prevent future awkwardness. It's terrible and I'm ashamed to admit it, but even with all my training and experience, I still allow people to isolate because it permits me to avoid a clumsy conversation. I know it's awkward and they know it's awkward, so I guess sometimes we just passively agree to avoid interacting.

Clearly, this isn't the right course of action, but perhaps seeing it laid out in black and white affords a bit of grace to those who have seemingly abandoned us after our loss. They don't necessarily want to leave us, but they are daunted by the circumstances and feel unequipped or foolish. Frankly, neither they nor we know exactly how to resume our casual relationship in the midst of grief.

During this awkward zone, reaching out to friends or doing things we used to enjoy may feel forced for a time. After all, wanting to interact with others and needing to interact with others are quite different. But in order to move forward after loss, we must push through the initial bumpy interactions and reconnect with our friends, family, work, hobbies, and faith. As we take those first uncomfortable steps, the activities become easier and help us to create new, positive, post-loss memories. These positive new memories become a kind of salve for the soul and help transform our wounds into scars.

Discover four other roadblocks that may be delaying the grieving process.

What ABOUT You?

Consider reaching out to someone this week to set up a phone chat, coffee, or outing for the sole purpose of reconnecting.

Even Jesus Wept

The shortest verse in the entire Bible is John 11:35. It simply says, "Jesus wept."

This verse isn't important because of its length but because it shows us something profound about the character of God. It may help us reframe the "why" questions that cause us to feel stuck.

If you aren't familiar with the story of a guy named Lazarus, you can find it in John chapter 11.

Lazarus is a close friend of Jesus and has fallen very sick. He's near death, so his sisters, Mary and Martha, send word to Jesus requesting help. Jesus, seemingly in no hurry to respond, gets the message, waits two days, and then heads their direction. But by the time he arrives, Lazarus has been dead four days. Mary and Martha had seen Jesus perform miracles before, so they knew that if he had wanted to, he could have healed Lazarus. But he delayed his trip, and now Lazarus is gone. Full of anger and disappointment, they protest the injustice of loss saying, "Master, if You had been here, my brother wouldn't have died!" (v. 21 TLV).

If the story ended there, we might be left picturing a heartless and cruel Jesus. Was he too busy performing other miracles that he couldn't make it in time? Could he not have just teleported himself to be with Lazarus and heal him? Martha and Mary may have had the same thoughts: "Why didn't you come to help us? We've seen you do miracles for people who have hardly any faith, and yet for your closest friends, you couldn't even come!"

Grief has this effect on most of us as well. We want answers. We want to understand why a good God would allow his children to suffer. Jesus, however, has a broader perspective—a different way of looking at things. He has a long-range plan in mind that we are unable to see. Halfway through the story, Jesus has already told Martha and his disciples that they are going to witness Lazarus being raised from the dead, but they all assume he's referring to the spiritual rebirth that will occur at the end of time. Little did they know that by raising Lazarus from the dead, Jesus would start a series of events that would change the world.

If you were to read John 12:42–53, you'd see how raising Lazarus instigated the attack on Jesus's life. The miracle of raising a man (not just healing him) who'd been dead for four days was so remarkable that it had everyone believing in Jesus. The religious men in power at the time were so threatened by his popularity that they began plotting to have him killed. This would eventually lead to the fulfillment of Jesus's entire purpose on earth: to die so that we might live. Mary and Martha couldn't see the bigger picture in the midst of their suffering, but Jesus could.

All of us would welcome the opportunity to see a miracle happen in our lives. And we believe that, deep down, all of us seek answers to deep truths about God. But few of us want to go to a deeper or more vulnerable situation to get there. Everyone wants to be saved from the lions, but few of us want to jump into the lions' den (see Daniel 6). Everyone wants to slay the giant, but few of us walk onto the field of battle with only a slingshot in our hands (see 1 Samuel 17).

In the story of Lazarus, Jesus was taking everyone present to a deeper level. He was showing them things about his character that they wouldn't have seen if he had simply healed Lazarus. He's doing the same with us. We're able to understand the characteristics of God because of the characteristics we see in Jesus. In this story, Jesus grieved. Put yourself in the shoes of Mary or Martha. You are standing there, watching the Savior of the world—the Son of God who was present at the creation of the earth—cry over the loss of your brother.

At first glance, you may think he was weeping primarily because he felt sad for his friends who didn't share his eternal perspective. And you would be right. However, there is more to it than that. He was profoundly moved in his spirit. He wasn't just shedding passive tears. Jesus was protesting the injustice of death itself. Death wasn't part of the original world God created for us to live in.

Instead of knowing loss, he wanted us to be whole, wanting for nothing. We were never meant to feel the deep ache of loss: the agonizing breathlessness after having the wind knocked out of us, the jarring silence of a song cut short.

We long for a world restored to its original state—richly abundant and void of death and decay. If you've been searching for answers to the "why" questions and deeply desire to understand the bigger picture, you aren't alone. As Paul says, "The whole creation has been groaning as in the pains of childbirth right up to the present time" (Rom. 8:22). We too groan for the restoration of all that has been lost, for a future that is not yet now. And this is the ultimate loss that happened in the garden: that there is absolute certainty of an uncertain future. We have lost, and even worse, we could lose again.

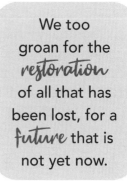

We too groan for the *restoration* of all that has been lost, for a *future* that is not yet now.

What ABOUT *You?*

Think about your loss. Put a name to it. Was it a person? Was it a marriage? Was it an ability? Don't limit your loss to just physical death. Was there a particular dream you once had that you gave up on because of your trauma? Was there a mindset or perspective that died as a result of your experiences? Did trauma change you, and you're grieving the loss of who you once were or who you hoped to become? Take a moment and write down your thoughts.

Next, think of when you lost it. Maybe it was in a single moment, or maybe it happened over time. Now picture Jesus right there with you as you lost it. He is standing beside you as you mourn that loss. He isn't watching with a cold heart; he is weeping with you. He is longing for perfection to be restored. He is longing to pull you close to his chest and remind you that this isn't the end, that there will be a resurrection, that death doesn't get the final say.

Just imagine Jesus saying, I cry over what you cry over. I hate that you had to experience this loss or any loss at all. I am here with you. I want to walk with you on your journey through grief. I am here to listen and to comfort. I am not as far away as you think. I love you and will stay with you always. This grieving process isn't a problem that needs to be fixed. It is a gift I gave you to help you heal. I know it is a heavy load to carry, so I will carry it with you.

Jesus wept for Lazarus. Jesus wept with Mary and Martha. And Jesus weeps with you. He wants to remind you that he is coming back to make all things new again. He'll revive what is dead and restore what is lost.

Moving from "Why" to "How" Questions

I (Evan) know, God knows, and you know that it can feel impossible to envision ever getting over a loss. Even the idea of moving forward might feel as if we have to leave the person or thing we loved behind. I'm not suggesting that acknowledging your grief and inviting others into the process instantly puts you on the fast track through it. In fact, I don't believe there is, or should even be, a fast track at all. This idea of getting over a loss is troubling to me because the journey through grief is less about *getting over* it and more about *moving through* it.

None of us could forget our loved one, and we wouldn't want to. But at the same time, we don't have to live with a permanently broken heart. There is a common misconception among grievers that "if I start moving through the grieving process, I will forget my loved one and their memory will fade." This mindset is bound to undermine the role of grief and may even limit the fond memories they can recall.[2]

The grieving process actually heightens the accuracy of our memories. We're able to see things from the past more vividly. We remember how something looked, smelled, or felt to the touch. This vivid crop of memories can be harvested to capture moments of deep meaning, joy, laughter, and love. It is possible to have both painful and pleasant memories at the same time. We can move forward without forgetting. In fact, talking about our memories, both painful and pleasant, helps us grieve. After trauma, we may feel numb and unable to describe the complex cocktail of emotions we are feeling. That's okay, and it's common. However, in spite of that numbness, those who are willing to begin talking about the circumstances of their loss will begin healing sooner.

You might say, "I'm just not ready to begin grieving yet." But think of it like this: if I was cooking dinner and cut my finger badly, blood would begin gushing out. What advice would you give me? You would advise me to seek immediate medical attention, right?

So if tragic circumstances broke my heart and I was emotionally bleeding, why would I delay? Shouldn't I attend to this wound immediately as well?

It's never too early to begin the grieving process. Let me say that again: it's *never* too early to begin the grieving process.

As I was writing this chapter, I called and texted a group of friends and former REBOOT participants about their approach to grief. Their answers were enlightening, to say the least. A recurring theme emerged that I think will be helpful for you.

We move forward on the path through grief when we replace the "why" questions with "how" questions:

- How can I build new dreams?
- How can I move forward?
- How can I deal with my pain and sense of loss?
- How can I get back to my former capacities?
- How can I learn through what I've experienced?

The "why" questions will likely send us chasing for answers that may never come. But the "how" questions can be answered. They look to the future rather than the past. They spark action rather than contemplation. They invite help from God and from others.

As I read the pathways my friends took through grief, their answers to the "how" questions were as varied as their personalities. Nathan chopped wood. Bob wrote in his journal. Lauren spoke out loud what she was going to miss and expressed her sadness over a future that would never be as she imagined. Austin went for a cross-country road trip by himself. Mary and Lloyd, Gold Star parents,[3] started a foundation and wrote a book to encourage military families suffering from PTSD. Ronne Rock, an author I admire, talked about how she learned to embrace grief as a friend rather than a problem to solve. Tammy bought a hydrangea, planted it in her backyard, and named it after the baby she had lost.

These actions were how my friends dealt with loss. In every case, they found ways to honor the people they lost with the lives they are now living. When they talk about their loved one, they speak about their life, not their death. My friends taught me that, while you may never "complete" your grief journey, you're nearing the end of it when you are able to think about the lost person more as a happy past memory than a painful present absence. They taught me that if you've lost something less tangible such as your security, ability, or self-worth, you're nearing the end of your grief journey when you have found purpose in what was lost and have adapted to it and are thriving in spite of it.

> We move **forward** on the path through grief when we **replace** the "why" questions with "how" questions.

They also taught me that while the time line for grief is different for every person, grieving is a process, not a permanent residence. So keep moving forward! My prayer is that as you carve your path on this journey, you'll start by asking your own "how" questions and continue by allowing God to reveal a way forward that is just right for you.

What ABOUT You?

Take ten minutes to brainstorm a list of activities you might like to try on your pathway through grief. Then pick a couple and set aside time this week to try them.

CHAPTER

six

Guilt, Shame, and Regret

*Moving Forward When You're
Stuck in the Past*

Setting the Record Straight

Ricky Jackson was eighteen years old when police arrested him
for the murder of Harold Franks. According to police, a pair of
assailants splashed acid on Franks's face, shot him several times,
and stole $425 before leaving the scene.[1] Ricky Jackson claimed his
innocence and had an alibi for his whereabouts during the crime.
But a twelve-year-old paperboy by the name of Eddie Vernon told
police he saw Jackson fire the gun that killed Harold Franks. His
testimony alone led to the conviction of Jackson, after which Jackson
son was sentenced to die by the electric chair. To most people,
the trial and verdict seemed fair. But there was one significant
problem: Eddie Vernon, the paperboy, didn't actually see anything
that happened that day.

In 2011, a Cleveland magazine published an article about the unstable nature of Jackson's conviction and the implausibility of the testimony that had condemned him. Among the readers was Eddie Vernon's pastor, who arranged a meeting between Vernon and lawyers with the Ohio Innocence Project. After the meeting, Vernon rescinded his 1975 testimony, saying he had been coerced into giving his previous statement. Finally, in 2014, prosecutors dismissed charges against Ricky Jackson—making him a free man after spending thirty-nine years behind bars for a crime he didn't commit.

Imagine for a moment that, despite his conviction being overturned, Jackson chose to stay locked up. Or even more counterintuitively, imagine that Jackson refused to believe that he was truly innocent. After all, he had spent nearly forty years living as a convicted man. Maybe he had simply grown accustomed to being viewed as a criminal. How devastating would that be? What a waste of life it would be! But that's exactly how many of us are living. We are doing time for a crime we didn't commit.

The goal of this chapter is to help you set the record straight. For some of us, that means we'll have to begin the process of making amends and righting our wrongs. For others, it will mean accepting our innocence and letting go of our guilt. Neither of these is an easy thing to do. Of the topics we've covered so far in this book, this subject can be one of the most threatening. We've literally had people yell at us in defense of their own guilt. Yes, you read that sentence right. They fought to stay condemned. They didn't want to hear anything about forgiveness or letting go. They were miserable, but in their minds, at least misery was familiar. They'd become so accustomed to life in their own emotional prison that they'd grown comfortable. Because the thought of leaving that prison felt overwhelming, they fought to stay locked up. We sure hope you won't do the same.

Remember that healing requires humility. So lower your defenses and open your heart. Freedom awaits.

What ABOUT You?

Have you ever fought to stay condemned even though others said it wasn't your fault? Why do you think we are often the hardest on ourselves?

The Triplets

Trauma robs us of our innocence and burdens us with guilt, shame, and regret. Remember that before Eve ate the apple, "Adam and his wife were both naked, and they felt no shame" (Gen. 2:25). While they were uncovered, they felt no shame because nothing sinful had ever happened. They were innocent, but that innocence was shattered when they ate from the tree of the knowledge of good and evil. By taking this knowledge for themselves, their eyes were opened to the reality of sin and its consequences. Similarly, our innocence was lost when sin and trauma intersected our lives. Guilt, shame, and regret invaded our minds and bodies and wounded our souls.

Guilt, shame, and regret, or the *triplets* as we call them, are among the most misunderstood and damaging emotions we experience. When the triplets are acting as they should, they help lead us toward what is true and what is right. However, when they're misbehaving, they can lead us into a depth of despair like no other.

In the end, guilt, shame, and regret will either help us move forward or leave us stuck, looking backward.

> In the end, guilt, shame, and regret will either help us move forward or leave us stuck, looking backward.

Of all the subjects that people ask me (Evan) about, this topic comes up most often. The triplets are masters of deception and will use any ambiguity in the facts to confuse us. The more confused we feel, the more open we become to their attack. Therefore, the only way I've found to fight back is to dismantle the triplets' logic, step by step, until I've answered the question Who is really at fault? Once I'm able to answer that question with absolute certainty, I can begin to heal.

A few weeks ago, I spoke to a room full of ER nurses, many with over fifteen years of experience in the field. These folks knew their stuff. Slightly intimidated, I had the inane thought that if there was ever a time for me to have a stroke or heart attack, this was the best place for it to happen. As I began sharing some of the content from this chapter, the tone of the room shifted. It was clear that I was hitting a nerve. For the next two hours, I listened as nurses shared heartbreaking stories of patients they had lost, and I watched with bewilderment as they questioned decisions they had made. Every story contained the words *I feel guilty* or *I regret*, and they showed themselves no mercy in their accusations against themselves. Though many of the experiences shared were from years ago, the nurses remembered the details as if they had just happened. That's probably because they had replayed these experiences hundreds of times in their heads, searching for a path to a better outcome. At one point, I asked the group what they did with these feelings, and they unanimously said they moved on and tried to make sure they never made the same mistakes again. On the surface, that sounded like they were repurposing the experience as a learning opportunity. But the subtext revealed that they believed they were to blame for losing the patient— something that was totally untrue in almost every case. This belief was eating away at them. Their families said they weren't the same anymore—they didn't smile and seemed detached and emotionally numb. On the other hand, the nurses felt ashamed of how they had let their careers impact their families. Not only had they let their patients down, but they were now letting their families down as well.

Now I'll ask you. Do you think they were right?

As an outsider, you can look at the situations and see that they did their best. You can confirm they made the choices that seemed right at the time, given the information they had. You can see how their career paths would put strain on even the strongest families. Chances are if you were sitting across from them right now, you would try to encourage them and tell them how thankful you are that people like them exist, people who are willing to answer the call to do a job few can do. Here's some foreshadowing: that's essentially what I'm going to do for you during this chapter. I'll be the one doing the encouraging, and you'll likely be saying some of the same things those nurses said. When you want to push back against my logic, I hope you'll remember this conversation and hear me out.

What ABOUT *You?*

When you read the words guilt, shame, and regret, which one stands out to you most? Why?

Guilt

Let's start by exploring *guilt*, the most judgmental of the triplets. Here's the way guilt should work: Do something wrong? Face the consequences.

If only it were that simple!

Guilt happens when we realize that we have violated our moral standards and take personal responsibility for that violation. In other words, we've done something wrong and we know it. Imagine you're a teenager, and you steal money from your dad's wallet. Even if you don't get caught, you may feel some level of guilt because you've broken a basic rule: don't steal. You knew stealing was wrong, but you did it anyway. The guilt we feel in this scenario is deserved. We earned it. There will be (and should be) consequences for our actions because we truly are guilty. This type of guilt serves a critical purpose in our lives. God gave us this feeling of guilt, or conviction, as a powerful preventative force—so much so that the avoidance of feeling guilty factors into our decision-making processes. Without much effort at all, I can think of ways that the memory of feeling guilty in the past has helped me avoid poor choices in the present. I'm betting you can as well. We think, *That felt terrible. I don't want to feel that again, so I'll choose differently this time.*

Second Corinthians 7:10 says, "Godly sorrow brings repentance that leads to salvation and leaves no regret, but worldly sorrow brings death." When we sin, we should feel godly sorrow, or guilt. This feeling of conviction is an internal alarm system telling us that we are out of bounds. Just as parents desire safety and well-being for their children, God also wants the best for us. When we play in the busy street instead of on the sidewalk, God shouts at us through his Holy Spirit to change our actions—leading us to repentance.

If you aren't familiar with the term *repentance*, or if you've only heard it used by fire-and-brimstone preachers, let me clarify it. It isn't merely behavior modification or self-control, although those may be signs of repentance. Repentance is less about stopping a certain action or set of actions and more about starting to follow Jesus again. It is saying, "I want to be more like Jesus in my thoughts, words, and actions." When functioning properly, guilt serves its purpose by leading us to repentance. So guilt not only helps us make better choices through repentance but also produces in us the kind of fruit we desire. We become more patient, kind, forgiving, disciplined, and honest.

But repentance isn't always so cut-and-dried because feeling guilty and being guilty are two different things.

We can feel guilty for almost anything, can't we? Eating that extra slice of cake, saying the wrong thing at the wrong time, not living up to our own expectations. The list of things we can feel guilty about is endless. But

> *Feeling* guilty and *being* guilty are two different things.

here's the point: we can feel guilty without having done anything wrong at all. That's how this member of the triplets misbehaves and wreaks havoc in our lives. It tells us we are guilty when in fact we are not. This is the trap of false guilt, and unlike true guilt, it isn't a gift from God.

False guilt tells us we deserve the misery we are facing even though we did nothing wrong. It carries with it a self-criticism designed to demoralize us. It ties us up in knots of complex emotions that are not easily sorted out. The more time that passes, the more tangled the knots. And the more tangled the knots, the more confused we become about what's fact and what's fiction. Bound up by the ropes of false guilt and mistrusting our own interpretations of the truth, too many of us are led toward a life of condemnation.

The word *condemnation* literally means to be sentenced to punishment. But what kind of punishment? How long should it last?

You see, while godly sorrow, or true guilt, leads us to repentance and restitution, false guilt leads us into a trap because there are no answers to the questions about the punishment. And here's the worst part: we believe that we fully deserve the punishment we are self-inflicting because we view ourselves as guilty. This sets the stage for shame, the second member of the triplets.

What ABOUT *You?*

How have feelings of guilt led to positive outcomes in your life? How have they led to negative outcomes?

Shame

Guilt says, "I did something bad."
Shame says, "I am bad."[2]

See the difference?

Shame says, "I let him touch me inappropriately, so I am dirty," or "I ignored the warning signs, so I am a bad parent." Shame is what happens when the guilt we feel—whether based on fact or not—shapes how we view ourselves. This member of the triplets loves to focus on blame. It doesn't judge merely the *actions* of individuals but the *individuals themselves*. Shame wants to determine specifically who is to blame and to convince that person they are nothing more than a collection of their mistakes and poor decisions.

People who feel ashamed will attribute virtually any negative outcome to a lurking sense of "badness" or deficiency they find in themselves. They think, *No matter what went wrong, it was probably my fault.* For those of us who have experienced trauma, this feeling can dominate our lives. If left unchecked, it will lead us to become resigned, depressed, and self-conscious. We will lower our expectations and give everyone grace except ourselves. And to make matters worse, shame will cause us to act in ways that produce more shame.

Notice the following two diagrams:

In the first diagram, our painful experiences point us toward (1) beliefs that produce (2) behaviors that bring about further

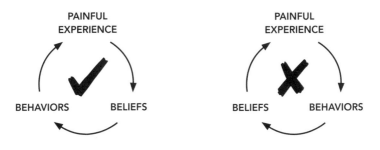

healing. It essentially illustrates that who we are will shape what we do. This is the ideal path. It's built on the foundation that says we all have intrinsic worth that cannot be diminished no matter what we do or what is done to us.

The second diagram recommends turning to behaviors in order to overcome challenges. It proposes that what we do will determine who we become. Work harder, take this medication, join the gym, see a counselor, and don't quit. It promises that doing these things will bring balance, success, and wellness. It's the foundational building block on which the self-help industry is based.

But there's a problem with the second way of thinking—and this is why shame is so important to our conversation about trauma: what we do doesn't determine who we are; who we are will determine what we do.

But since shame says that we are bad, we will act bad. If we see ourselves as guilty, convicted, or condemned, we will often behave in a manner congruent with these beliefs. Self-harm, drug abuse, promiscuity, isolation, alcohol abuse, and suicide become more appealing through the lens of shame. And as we deal with the fallout from these poor choices, we pile on more guilt, creating an ideal environment for shame to compound.

> **What we do doesn't determine who we are; *who* we are will determine *what* we do.**

Shame doesn't present itself right away. It is sneaky and sly. Our home has a beautiful master bathroom. Honestly, the shower is better than most fancy hotel showers. But cleaning the grout around the tile is the absolute worst. The mildew builds up slowly, and by the time I notice, it's gross and spread all over. Shame is like mildew. It builds slowly over time. The longer false guilt sits on the surface, the more shame grows underneath. And the more shame grows, the more self-loathing and self-inflicted punishment we feel we deserve.

To put it another way, shame adds time to our sentence by denying us the freedom to which we are entitled.

What ABOUT *You?*

How has shame influenced your behavior?

Regret

As shame grows, the third triplet jumps into the mix. We sit condemned to ever-expanding self-punishment while the rest of the world moves on without us. Until one day we wake up full of regret, wishing we had done things differently. Wishing we had made different decisions or seen the truth sooner. By the time we feel regret, it's too late. What's done is done.

The underpinning of regret is comparison. We compare what we wished had happened to what actually happened. We call regret the "worst feeling of all the feelings" because of the way it attacks our complete personhood. Regret hammers our self-esteem into self-pity. It makes us doubt our decision-making abilities and can completely paralyze us from making progress.

Remember how I said that guilt, shame, and regret can leave us stuck, looking backward? Regret is the backward-looking part. It is nearly impossible to experience freedom and joy in the present if we are plagued by regrets of the past. There are two kinds of regret:

1. Regret of omission—things we didn't do that we wish we had done.
2. Regret of commission—things we did that we wish we hadn't done.

Regrets of omission are often linked to false guilt and shame while regrets of commission are usually linked to true guilt and conviction. Either way, regret is such a terrible feeling that we aren't likely to forget the choices we end up regretting. The desire to avoid regret may lead us to filter our present and future decisions through a regret-prevention mindset. Thoughts such as *What if I do this and something bad happens?* become a common internal debate. Over the last few years, I've noticed the regret-prevention mindset is becoming more common. We all want to avoid painful or traumatic experiences. Perhaps, after a specific event, we vow to never let something like it happen again.

- He pledges to never invest in another business again after his company goes under.
- She vows to never fall in love again after a traumatic divorce from a narcissist.
- He promises to never put his kids in a situation where they could be sexually abused the way he was.

The idea here is to avoid doing anything we might regret later. I get it, but here's the ironic part: if you avoid doing anything you might regret later, you'll avoid doing anything that has any degree of risk—which is almost everything.

Yes, he never invested and took a risk in business again, but he sat on several brilliant ideas and he'll never know what could have become of them. Yes, she never fell in love with a narcissist again, but she also never had another romantic relationship. Yes, he never put his kids in a situation where they could be abused, but his children never got to know their grandparents or neighbors very well and his suspicious mindset was passed on to them. Avoiding the risk of regret will cause you to disengage from opportunities, companionship, family, activities, and eventually life itself—and there is no greater regret than that!

> If you avoid doing anything you might *regret* later, you'll avoid doing *anything* that has any degree of risk—which is almost *everything*.

The triplet of regret misbehaves when it causes us to fear making mistakes. This fear makes healing nearly impossible because there's no perfect path through healing. Therefore, regret is a life-limiting threat. It lures us into comparing the risks of an unknown future with a known past. We get stuck looking backward because at least we have learned, to some degree, how to cope with the past. But we never get to discover the potential joy of the future. It blocks us from becoming who we can become and doing what we can do by keeping us pointed in the wrong direction, the only direction we truly can't change. We can't change the past, yet we become defined by it. As Sissy Gavrilaki says, "When the past becomes your present, you lose your future."[3]

Perhaps you feel like you've lost your future. We'll admit, there have been times when we were unable or unwilling to look forward. It was just too painful to risk dreaming, hoping, or wishing for something better. At the start of this book, we said that healing from trauma ends in empowerment—empowerment to move forward in spite of the past and empowerment to help others by sharing our unique stories. We defined that as our destination. This is the forward part.

Shake off the regret. It is in the past. You've grown. The fact that you feel regret is a sign of your maturity. God is working things out in you. Yes, you may mess up again along the way. That's OK. You aren't perfect, but God is. So let him finish his work in you.

What ABOUT You?

What regrets do you have about your life since the trauma(s) occurred?

Putting the "Triplets" on Trial

A Few Good Men is perhaps my (Evan's) favorite movie. I'm such a sucker for courtroom dramas! We all know the intense scene as the lawyers present their cases and, after the closing arguments conclude, the jury is dismissed to decide a verdict. We're then taken to a private room where we see the jurors carefully reviewing the evidence and the testimony of witnesses. They consider the motive and the character of the plaintiff, and they ask themselves if the accused is guilty beyond reasonable doubt.

In a courtroom, the truth is paramount. The final goal of any trial is to identify the truth and to administer justice accordingly. That's what we are going to do now. We are going to put your guilt, shame, and regret on trial. We'll examine the accusations against you, review the facts, and issue a ruling.

Here are the three stages of this process:

1. Accusation—What do "they" say you did or didn't do?
2. Trial—What are the facts of the case?
3. Ruling and Sentencing—Are you guilty or not guilty, and who should pay for the crimes committed?

Let's see what the truth has to say about your situation. We've included some blank lines for you to write your answers to the questions below. Please don't just read through this in order to finish the chapter. If you aren't in the headspace or don't have the time to dive into this right now, consider taking a break and coming back to it when you do have the time. This is a chain-breaking activity and is worthy of your attention.

Accusation

First, we'll consider the accusations. What are you being accused of or what are you accusing yourself of? What are others—or the voices in your head—saying you did or didn't do? Are they saying "you did a bad thing," or are they telling you "you are bad"? What are the "should've," "would've," and "could've" statements that you hear playing in your head as you lie down at night?

Many of the people we've worked with over the years have had to realize that the only ones accusing them were themselves. In their courtroom, it was them against them. Maybe the same can be said about you. Take plenty of time to write out the accusations you've felt or heard. The next step will wait until you are ready.

_____

_____

_____

_____

_____

Trial

Next, we move into the trial phase. This is where we look at the evidence of what really happened. As we've said earlier, we can't always trust our feelings. We must let facts influence our emotions rather than the other way around. So what are the facts of your case?

Did you knowingly cause harm to others or yourself? Are the facts against you being mishandled or misinterpreted? Did your actions break God's commandments? Are the facts pointing toward truly poor decisions you made, or do they point toward lose-lose scenarios where only in hindsight can you identify better solutions? Are the facts manipulating you into blaming yourself for crimes committed by others?

Really take some time to logically think through your feelings. It may even help to envision yourself in a courtroom, defending yourself or accusing the actual wrongdoer. Yes, a bad thing happened, but are you bad?

Any courtroom drama worth watching has a slick lawyer. These silver-tongued fast talkers attempt to mislead the jury through clever courtroom trickery. They spin the facts and distort the truth to get people to see what they want them to see rather than what is truly there. When we've walked through this trial activity with groups of trauma survivors, usually about nine out of ten of them acknowledge that they've fallen for a courtroom trick. Their accusers have attempted to place blame on them rather than on the actual cause of the trauma. These courtroom tricks are meant to bring false guilt, shame, and regret. And the truth is they work unless they are called out for what they are. Following are some of the most common tricks. See if you relate to any of the false accusations or the false beliefs about yourself that accompany them. And remember, these are *tricks*. They are 100 percent false. Do not let the facts of your case be distorted by these deceptions.

You should have fought back more.

- "I didn't stop the abuse from happening, and I didn't tell anybody about the abuse when I had the chance. Doesn't this 'prove' I wanted the abuse to continue?"

- "My body responded to the sexual abuse. That 'proves' that I must have wanted it to happen."
- "I stayed in the relationship and didn't stand up for myself. I guess anyone dumb enough to stay in a bad situation deserves what happens to them."

It was your responsibility.

- "It was my job to protect my baby. If I had known what signs to look for, I would have gone to the hospital and my baby would be alive today."
- "I was driving the car. It was my job to keep everyone safe, and I didn't do it."
- "I enabled them to keep using drugs. It was my fault that they became an addict."

You're guilty by association.

- "I chose to be around those people, so when that terrible thing happened, it was my fault for being there."

You may have felt helpless, but you could have controlled the situation.

- "I wanted to help him, but I couldn't get him to listen to me, and he ended up taking his own life. How can I live with myself?"
- "I wanted to stop cutting myself, but I just couldn't."
- "I knew he was cheating on me, but I stayed anyway. I'm so foolish."

There were other options; you just weren't trying hard enough.

- "If I stayed, I could've ended up in a harmful situation. But if I left, I'd be leaving someone I cared about. I was forced to make a lose-lose choice."
- "Even though my parents didn't believe me, I should have told the police what my neighbor was doing to me."

We'll keep moving through this activity for now and circle back to the courtroom tricks in the next lesson.

What ABOUT You?

Take a few minutes to write out the accusations you've heard and the facts of your case.

Ruling and Sentencing

Let's shift to the ruling and sentencing stages where we'll determine if you are in fact guilty or not guilty of wrongdoing. This should, from a purely logical perspective at least, help determine if the guilt, shame, and regret you feel are helping you move forward or keeping you stuck, looking backward.

Some of us may look at our situations and identify actual wrongdoing. In other words, we did the crime. We knowingly hurt another or ourselves. We broke the law, broke our word, or broke someone's heart. If that's the case for you, you may be feeling godly sorrow. Recall that godly sorrow leads to repentance, and repentance means that you can change.

We've worked with men who were abused as children and became abusers when they had children of their own. During our conversations, they lamented over their actions. What they were feeling was more than regret; it was remorse.

Regret is feeling bad about things that did or did not happen in the past.

Remorse is allowing that regret to change our behavior in the future.

We find that *remorse* conveys a deeper, more profound feeling than *regret*. For example, when we decline an invitation to dinner or a party, we send our regrets. We'd never say, "I send my remorse." On the other hand, in courtrooms, when guilty persons are scrutinized for evidence of self-awareness and acknowledgment of their crimes, we look for signs of remorse, not signs of regret. A criminal may *regret* being caught, but justice demands their *remorse*. We are looking for them to take ownership of their wrongdoing and the harm they caused.

Remorse happens when regret, caused by godly sorrow, yields the healthy fruit of repentance. If your trial ended with conviction, consider if you have shown remorse or merely regret. Are you allowing these feelings to bring about a repentant future?

In the earthly criminal justice system, the convicted are sent to prison to give them time to experience regret, remorse, and isolation from the outside world. But in the spiritual realm, Jesus took our punishment and now offers us his unblemished, spotless record. Remember that "godly sorrow brings repentance that leads to salvation and leaves no regret" (2 Cor. 7:10). Romans 3:23–24 says, "For all have sinned and fall short of the glory of God, and all are justified freely by his grace through the redemption that came by Christ Jesus." The word *justified* in this verse could be rephrased as "just as if you had never sinned."

Christ offers to do the time for the crimes we've committed. He offers us freedom in spite of our wrongdoing. If you're feeling the weight of conviction right now, know that through Jesus, God isn't mad at you, and he isn't condemning you to a life of self-inflicted punishment. We'll talk more about forgiveness later in the book, but remember that guilt, shame, regret, and remorse for true guilt should function to help us move forward. If they aren't doing this, we may find we have a misunderstanding of forgiveness.

But some of us are more like Ricky Jackson. We've been falsely accused, and we've come to accept a verdict of guilty even though we are innocent. This "worldly sorrow" leads to death. Things die when we get stuck looking backward. We give up on dreams and our relationships rot. Did you know that in Revelation 12:10, Satan is called the "accuser"? The book of John says, "He was a murderer from the beginning, not holding to the truth, for there is no truth in him. When he lies, he speaks his native language, for he is a liar and the father of lies" (8:44).

Satan is the originator of lies. He is your enemy, and his battle-field is your mind. His goal is to devour you. He knows your vulner-abilities and past traumas. He'll exploit any weakness he can find. He wants you to rehash every memory, overanalyze it, and put a magnifying glass on anything that could be construed as a misstep on your part. He knows you are your own toughest critic. The longer you listen to his lies, the more familiar and believable they become. And if you aren't careful, before long you won't be able to distinguish between your voice and the lies he whispers to you. We've seen Satan's lies delay healing for so many people:

- The mother who blames herself for the miscarriage of her child.
- The son who believes he provoked the abuse he received.
- The teen who makes excuses for the person who sexually abused her.
- The divorcee who blames herself for not getting out of the abusive marriage sooner.
- The clinician who mercilessly beats himself up for not seeing the warning signs before his client's suicide.
- The parents who feel responsible for not recognizing the addictive behaviors developing in their child.
- The driver who accidentally hits a pedestrian walking on the side of the road on a dark, rainy night.

In each of these scenarios and in thousands more like them, the "should'ves" and "could'ves" don't stack up to the facts. The "why" and "if only" statements are dead-end roads. Sure, in hindsight we might wish we had changed the way we handled a situation. But we can't change it now, and we couldn't have changed it in the moment either. A jury of our peers would examine the evidence and declare us not guilty, and yet we feel condemned. We can know we are trapped in false guilt when the evidence of our innocence isn't enough to change how we feel. The courtroom tricks may have worked in the past, but they don't have to work anymore.

You should have fought back more.

Humans react to threats through the fight, flight, or freeze response. If you were a child, were overpowered, or had limited resources at your disposal, two of those options were off the table. You couldn't fight back, and even if you tried to flee, maybe you had nowhere to go. So you endured it. Perhaps your body did respond to the sexual abuse. That was a physiological response that was out of your control. Maybe you did willingly go back to the abuser's house again or stay in the abusive relationship, but at the time, you weren't in a clear frame of mind due to the emotional, mental, or physical abuse you were experiencing. You made the best choices with the options and information you had at the time.

It was your responsibility.

It is impossible to keep yourself and those around you safe at all times. Every day, you put yourself in life-threatening situations whether or not they appear that way at the time. With life's countless moving parts, the potential for disaster is ever-present. You are not God, and you cannot control all the variables simultaneously. Tragedies happen. What you experienced was terrible, but it wasn't your fault.

You're guilty by association.

Psychologists often call this the "association fallacy." Did you have the power to authorize the abuse? Did you have the influence to stop it? Being around someone who is guilty doesn't make you guilty if you didn't participate in the abuse.

You may have felt helpless, but you could have controlled the situation. There were other options; you just weren't trying hard enough.

The "if onlys" of this kind of guilt are irrelevant. In hindsight, we may be able to see other options (or not), but in the moment of crisis, no one can see them all. You did your best at that moment under those conditions, and no one can judge you for it. You may wish that some magical solution would have presented itself in real time, but it didn't. That's reality, and it's not your fault.

This isn't an exhaustive list of false-guilt tricks, so you may want to write a response poking holes in the specific lie you heard. And remember, often these lies aren't just all in your head. Sometimes they are echoes of actual voices you've heard—accusations made by loved ones you thought were on your side. In all of these cases, it's normal to feel sad, angry, and frustrated about how things turned out. But don't turn your emotions in on yourself. You weren't meant to take the hit for those very unfair and unfortunate events—so don't take it. The only way to deal with false guilt is to recognize it as false, illogical, and irrational; shine a spotlight on its source; and ask God to remove it from you. The feelings of guilt, shame, and regret may not lift immediately, but keep bringing them before God and let him take the burdens off your shoulders.

True guilt leads to growth. False guilt leads only to pain and suffering. God doesn't mean for you to carry the burden of false guilt. No one else wants you to either. Will you lay it down?

From guilt to shame to regret is the path too many of us have taken over the years. But here's what we've found: there's no joy found in regret, there's no purpose found in shame, and there's no restoration found in just *feeling* guilty.

Trauma may have robbed you of your innocence, but don't let it declare you guilty.

What ABOUT You?

What was the verdict of your "trial"? Which, if any, courtroom tricks have you experienced that have distorted the truth of your situation? How did this chapter allow you to see your guilt, shame, and regret from a different perspective?

CHAPTER seven

Rejection, Neglect, and Abandonment

*Knowing You're Worthy When
You Feel Worthless*

Rejection

I wonder what it would feel like to have absolute approval, void of any insecurities? I can hardly imagine. I guess it's time for another episode of *Things I Can't Believe I'm Sharing in This Book* with your host, Evan. The truth is I care deeply about what others think of me. I want to be thought of as smart, funny, and kind. I want to feel like I have a "seat at the table"—while still reserving a seat at all of the other tables in the room at the same time! I like to be liked. I want to be accepted, especially by the people who seem least likely to accept me.

This drive in my life hasn't been easy to overcome. For someone who craves acceptance, the opportunity for rejection is everywhere:

They didn't share my post. Rejected.

I got turned down for a promotion. Rejected.

He didn't call me back after my second voicemail. Rejected.

My friends went to lunch and didn't invite me. Rejected.

It seems the more importance I place on acceptance, the more often I feel rejected.

In my experience, rejection from others hurts, but what follows hurts more. The self-criticism and play-by-play analysis of my actions causes the most damage. I can hear the words I say to myself even as I write this: *Evan, you weren't friendly enough. You didn't ask enough interesting questions. You've gained weight and everyone noticed. You weren't successful enough to be in that room. Those people were way out of your league.*

Time and time again, my endless pursuit of approval from others has ended in hurt, anxiety, and anger. But I'm lucky. The people rejecting me don't matter all that much in the grand scheme of things. They aren't my parents, my wife, or my kids. They're just people—the kind who will come and go.

Rejection from someone closer, like a family member, is a far deeper hurt. It's one thing to feel unwelcome or overlooked by an acquaintance; it's quite another to be denied or refused by someone we love. This kind of rejection shakes us to our core because it's by the people who should be most accepting of us. It sends the message that we aren't important or at least not important enough. So we journey down a dark hole of self-analysis, looking for whatever flaws make us unworthy of their care and attention. We feel like a burden to others. We think, *Maybe if I can change this or that, then they'll love me.*

On and on, we dance to the incessant drumbeat of self-critique. As one of my friends said to me one day, "How can I expect anyone else to love me if even my own parents didn't?"

The most damaging consequence of rejection by others is the rejection of ourselves that follows. No one's words or actions can hurt us more than our own. They limit our potential and rob us of opportunities.

Self-criticism can make us our own worst enemy. We may find ourselves having persistent feelings of loneliness or unworthiness. We may become overly affectionate toward people we hardly know and yet emotionally isolate from those closest to us. We may feel a constant insecurity or even a form of *rejection paranoia*, the fear that if others get too close, they will reject us as we've been rejected in the past. So we deflect rejection by avoiding the vulnerability required for deep friendship. In some cases, we may even begin to see ourselves as charity cases and take whatever others will give us, even if the attention is unhealthy or abusive.

> The most *damaging* consequence of rejection by others is the *rejection* of ourselves that follows. No one's words or actions can hurt us more than our *own*.

One of my good friends, Jess, has experienced rejection. Growing up in a house of seven children, she quickly learned that her father didn't like her. In fact, he told her so to her face. As a young girl she was talented and smart yet never got praise. She would seek affirmation or physical reassurance and be met with an uninterested stare. She saw him every day, and every day he made a hurtful choice to dismiss her. It was cruel. Every interaction was another slice by the blade of rejection. Others in her family seemed to get along with her dad just fine. But for whatever reason, she never seemed to be accepted by him.

It's funny, because she is one of the easiest people to get along with that I've ever met. Yet when Jenny and I first started spending time with her, we had to remind her that we actually liked hanging out with her. She would say things like "Well, I better go. I know I've overstayed my welcome," or "I'll just finish this slice of pizza and get out of your hair." In her mind, we were counting down the minutes until we were rid of her annoying presence. Nothing could have been further from the truth, but the repeated rejection and neglect she experienced growing up led to an insecurity and fear that other people are just too nice or too passive to tell her what they really think.

Thankfully, Jess is healing from the wound of rejection. And watching her grow in confidence over the past several years has been like watching a dormant tree come into season. All the creativity, passion, and talent that had been suppressed by rejection are blossoming before our very eyes. Jess, if you are reading this book, for real, we enjoy having you around!

That goes for you too. You aren't a charity case. People enjoy having you around. What I wouldn't give to feel fully accepted without any insecurity. But I'm not quite there yet. So in the meantime, I'm adopting a zero-tolerance policy on self-criticism.

Too many times, I've allowed what other people think of me to influence what I think of myself. No more! Instead, I'm learning to express gratitude for the people in my life who allow me to be myself. I'm starting to see rejection as a gift from God in that he saved me the time and energy of investing in a relationship with someone who would eventually hurt me. I'm also learning to form deeper relationships with a smaller group of people who truly know me and love me in spite of my flaws. The end result is that I don't worry as much about what anyone else thinks. I invite you to do the same.

Meet Jess and hear her encouragement for you.

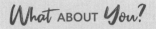

Who in your life has shown you acceptance? What did it look like? How can you seek out others who will do the same?

Neglect

We've all been rejected at one point or another in our lives. But some of us have faced a repeated rejection known as *neglect*. Neglect is what happens when we are not cared for properly. It's when the people who are supposed to provide us love and safety fail to do so:

A parent who fails to change their child's diaper.

An adult who is too busy to take care of their aging parent.

A husband who is too wrapped up in his work to notice his wife's pain.

A mother who never tells her kids they did a good job.

These are the traumas of neglect. They are passive forms of abuse in which the damage is done through inaction, indifference, and self-absorption.

Most people think of trauma as the result of a bad thing happening to them. But in my experience, some of the most devastating traumas aren't caused by a bad thing happening at all. They are caused by a good thing—a necessary thing—not happening.

My friend Karen was raised in a home with two drug abusers. Every Friday night they would take her to the attic and slide the lock shut. They told her that they were doing it for her own good so that she wouldn't be in any danger. Through the insulation and drywall, she could hear the loud music and rantings of drunk and high adults. Friends and neighbors snorted lines of cocaine and partied until they passed out. Eventually, sometimes nearly a day later, her parents would come to get her and she'd help them clean up the mess. As she got older, they didn't lock her in the attic; instead they had her help them draw lines of cocaine when they had become too high to do it themselves. Her parents failed to provide the safety and security she needed. They neglected her. Their neglect led to sexual abuse, suicide attempts, and chronic self-doubt.

Nobody deserves to be neglected. Hear me clearly: you weren't neglected because of your actions. You were neglected because of someone else's failure to act. That wasn't your fault. You were good enough to deserve attention. You were worthy to be loved. Your needs mattered then, and they matter now.

Isaiah 53:3 tells us that Jesus was "rejected by mankind, a man of suffering, and familiar with pain. Like one from whom people hide their faces he was despised."

God knows all about rejection and neglect. While your earthly father, mother, and even so-called friends may have rejected you, God chose you. And he chooses you again and again and again.

The next time you feel rejected or neglected, remember that you've been selected. You've been chosen by the most powerful and important being in the universe. And no matter what you do, there's nothing that will ever make him stop loving you.

Ever.

A couple years ago, Karen completed a REBOOT course and finally embraced her identity as a chosen, dearly loved child of God. But she didn't stop there! She completed another course and then another. Then she started volunteering and got trained to lead her own course. She's going out into her community and personally inviting people who have been rejected, overlooked, and neglected to reclaim their true identity too. Who knows, maybe this is her way of inviting you right now.

Meet Karen and hear the amazing story of how God is using her today!

What, if any, good and necessary things did not happen in your early life? How has this impacted you as an adult?

Abandonment

Abandonment is total and permanent neglect.

It's a "super wound" powered by chronic rejection that leaves an unfillable void in its wake. We see it in the child who has to raise themselves from an early age or the spouse who has to pick up the pieces after their partner walks out, never to be seen again. Abandoned is what we feel when someone we love chooses to neglect us forever.

If you've been abandoned, here's something we want you to know: you've suffered a loss, and just like any other loss, you need to grieve it. Grieving someone who willingly abandoned us seems like the last thing we'd ever want to do, but it's vitally important. Regardless of how our relationship was at the time they left us, we are still emotionally connected to them. We have a history, even if that history mostly consists of our unmet hopes and expectations. So whether we love them or hate them (or a mixture of both), we must grieve them. If we don't, our unprocessed grief will manifest in the form of strong, unpredictable emotions, physical health problems, and unstable future relationships. If the process of grieving and mourning is a challenge, take some time to revisit chapter 5.

We all respond differently to abandonment. Some of us become people pleasers. We do whatever it takes to keep loved ones in our lives even if it means enduring neglect, unhappiness, loneliness, or even abuse. No matter how toxic our relationships become, we will not be the ones who end them. Others of us isolate ourselves as a means of protection. In essence, we hedge against the risk of abandonment by keeping our distance. Our motto becomes Trust No One, Never Get Hurt. We're suspicious of anyone who seeks to be our ally. We wonder, *What's in it for them?* We no longer fear having to fend for ourselves because we've been there and done that. Now our greatest fear is being hurt again. We figure no one can abandon us if we never rely on them. Logically, this gives us the upper hand and reduces our vulnerabilities. But emotionally, we become an island unto ourselves. Sure, we may have relationships, but we miss out on the intimacy of real trust. We won't be taken advantage of or abandoned, but we'll be alone. I'm not sure which is worse.

My (Evan's) childhood friend Blake was six when his dad walked out. His mom was left with two children to feed and a lot of unanswerable questions. She worked hard to keep things together, but as I got older, I noticed that Blake didn't seem to handle his dad leaving very well. He was angry, unpredictable, and violent. My dad recognized the void that his father had left, so he tried to give him experiences that a father should give their child. One time we brought Blake with us to the zoo. We had a great time. He smiled nearly the entire trip. Looking back, it is one of my favorite childhood memories. Yet only a few days later, during a game of pickup basketball, Blake lost his temper. Before I knew it, he was beating me up for no apparent reason.

Another time, my dad helped us build an amazing fort in the woods behind our house. Blake seemed genuinely grateful for my dad's mentorship and guidance. But again, the next day his anger got the best of him, and he went out back and destroyed the fort. As a young boy, I never understood why he took his anger out on me. I mean, I wasn't the one who left him. But now I understand that I had a dad who stayed, and the constant comparison triggered a lot of anger in Blake.

I'd love to tell you that Blake learned to cope with his loss, but he didn't. He began using and selling drugs and has been in and out of jail a few times. He had a chance to trust my dad, who was more than willing to help guide him into manhood. But he got stuck in his anger and resentment and never moved through the grieving process.

Let's not do that. Instead, let's learn how to trust people again.

But how? Every relationship worth keeping relies on trust. Putting trust in anything or anyone requires risk, and most of us have a fairly low risk tolerance. So how can we reduce the risk of getting hurt while simultaneously starting to trust again?

First, make the choice to slowly increase your risk tolerance. You don't have to dive headfirst into a new relationship. You can (and should) start slow. Begin by sharing some vulnerable bits of information about yourself at each interaction. See if the other person responds in a way that is emotionally supportive and helpful. If they do, share a bit more.

Second, intercept unhelpful thoughts as they happen. If you find yourself thinking *They won't be there for me when I need them most*, pause for a moment and examine that thought. Is it true? Is there any evidence to back up that belief, or are you letting past trauma poison a potentially healthy relationship?

Last, branch out! No one person can or should be your entire support system. When someone stepped into a relationship with you, they didn't commit to being your only lifeline. Don't ask others to do for you what they are unable to offer to anyone. It is likely that they don't have the capacity, skills, or experience to be your sole support system. They didn't sign up for that, so don't expect it from them. Invite others into your circle.

When your trust in humankind has been broken, trusting anything or anyone can feel downright foolish. It's risky to rely on others when you've been fending for yourself for so long. Yeah, you've gotten by. You've made it on your own. That's something to be proud of. But it isn't something you can do forever. I can't promise you that you'll never be abandoned again. But I can promise you that if you don't learn to trust again, you'll find yourself just as alone as if you were abandoned. So grieve, get angry, and then give people a chance. They may surprise you.

What ABOUT *You?*

How has abandonment shaped how you view yourself, God, and other people? Who in your life can you trust right now? What makes them trustworthy?

Establishing Loving, Trusting Relationships

Here's something we probably don't want to think about. The same people who rejected, neglected, and abandoned us (if they are still living) may currently be in relationships with others. They may be dating someone, married, or raising children. But at this moment, they are likely actively bringing their woundedness and dysfunction into those relationships.

We don't want to do that. We want to build relationships that are marked by mutual respect, honesty, trust, and kindness. We don't want to reject others or be suspicious of everyone we encounter.

The *you* that you bring to any relationship needs to be whole and healthy for the relationship to flourish. I'll be the first to admit that this isn't easy, but it is possible. And it starts with healing the wound of rejection by claiming your true identity.

Recall that before the trauma of sin, Adam and Eve had an untarnished sense of self-worth and belonging. They saw themselves only through the eyes of God and knew that they were wholly loved and accepted.

Similarly, as children we see ourselves through our parents' eyes. We trust their interpretation of reality. This is problematic when our parents are neglectful or hypercritical of us. Early on, we adopt a distorted view of our worth, and this defines who we grow to become. At some point in our adulthood, however (maybe this is happening to you right now), we take off the tinted glasses and begin to see ourselves and our parents as we and they truly are. We begin to see that their rejection of us had everything to do with *them*—their mental illness, shame, sin, or personal struggles—and nothing to do with us. We were rejected because they had unhealed wounds. Hurt people hurt people. We just happened to be one of the ones they hurt.

Thank God that our parents don't get the final say on our worth as adults! But you might be surprised to read that we don't either.

The only one who has a definitive say in assigning our worth is the one who created us. And as you'll read in a later chapter, your worth is beyond measure. Knowing this is vitally important because, in my experience, we can only truly heal the wounds of rejection, neglect, and abandonment when we embrace God's view of our identity by getting to know him as the loving and compassionate Father he is. This relationship with God and Creator becomes the bedrock on which all our human relationships are built.

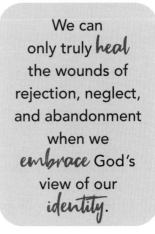

We can only truly *heal* the wounds of rejection, neglect, and abandonment when we *embrace* God's view of our *identity*.

I (Jenny) met Brandon at the occupational therapy clinic at Fort Campbell. He had a reputation of being challenging to work with because he questioned everything and didn't settle for any bs. I'd had difficult patients before, so I was not fazed when Brandon waddled into the treatment room (on top of his traumatic brain injury, he also had some orthopedic and nerve damage issues that caused him severe pain), eased into a chair, and said something semioffensive to break the ice.

Brandon was like so many people we encountered over the years. His hardened exterior and callous attitude were developed over years of self-preservation. You see, Brandon witnessed his father's suicide when he was five years old. He also processed the remains of a friend and fellow soldier who was burned alive when her Humvee was hit by a roadside bomb in Iraq. Brandon knew the deep wound of being abandoned by his earthly father. And what he experienced in combat only solidified his belief that no heavenly Father was going to reach down and save him. He was on his own, and that meant he had to be meaner and stronger than any threat he was up against.

Thankfully, I didn't pose much of a threat. But what I did do was build a friendship with Brandon. He and Evan and I began spending time together on the weekends. He took us skeet shooting and helped Evan install a car stereo. I made him hot chocolate with homemade whipped cream, and Evan took him suit shopping. Eventually he came to REBOOT and joined us at church.

The key to Brandon's healing was that he began to see the hand and feel the love of God in his life. He realized that he had never truly been abandoned and that God had been with him all along. At the end of REBOOT, Brandon described himself like a Cadbury cream egg: a hard shell on the outside but gooey and sweet on the inside. I'm smiling just recalling this because Brandon was as honest as they get. He was a straight shooter. He went to God with his anger and his mess and he found peace. He found his true identity. He wasn't the unwanted little boy or the disgruntled veteran. He was a child of God.

Brandon's story didn't end there. Once he began healing the wound of abandonment, Brandon found his superpower: reaching out to other people. Brandon can talk to anybody—and he will! He became our local outreach coordinator and began drawing other soldiers to the course. Once he experienced the love and trustworthiness of God, he began to extend love and trust to other people.

If your life has been overshadowed by the wounds of rejection, neglect, or abandonment, extending yourself to others can be daunting. Like Brandon, you may have a protective exterior that needs to be stripped away first. Or you may feel too vulnerable to risk being disregarded again. But consider that there is a huge population of people just like you who have experienced similar wounds and who are trying to find authentic, loving, and trusting relationships. Like Brandon, seek out these people and heal together!

Evan and I have often joked that people oversell the value of our curriculum. The truth is I'm pretty certain we could all get together every week and play Ping-Pong for an hour and healing would occur as long as everyone was there to truly heal and connect. We teach all of our trauma-healing course leaders that we are a community first and a course second. People may come for the content initially, but they stay for the community. So as much as reading this book will help, I can't overemphasize the necessity of getting in a group. After more than a decade of working in trauma care, I'm more convinced than ever that loving, trusting relationships are the backbone of long-term emotional, mental, and spiritual health. I hope you'll go start building some today.

Meet Brandon and hear how he was able to help Evan and Jenny through their own trauma.

What ABOUT You?

Imagine your life five years from now. You've experienced significant healing, and you've started building healthy relationships. What do these relationships look like?

Hurt and Abuse

Finding Peace When Your Life Is Full of Fear

When Home Feels like Hell

"It's time to go home!" I (Evan) hollered to our kids, who were getting in one last swim before the long drive home from Jekyll Island, Georgia. We were all sad to see our vacation come to an end, but we were also ready to be back in our own beds and into some sense of routine. Well, at least Mom and Dad were. I mean, can you even call it a vacation when you take three boys under the age of seven with you?

Whether it's after a long day at work or a tiresome road trip, there's nothing quite like walking through the door of our home. The smell, the familiarity, and the ability to relax all blend together to create a sense of peace and comfort. Among the things we love about our home, perhaps our most treasured possession in life, is our mattress. We genuinely cherish our mattress! Granted, it wasn't cheap, but it has been worth every single penny. With it, we purchased some fancy memory foam pillows. Y'all, these pillows are special. Most people sit on their couch or recliner at night. Jenny and I sit on our bed. If you think this is strange, it's because you haven't found the right bed yet.

We love coming home because our home is a place where we are free to be ourselves and where there are no expectations on us other than adhering to our basic family values. Our home has plenty of laughs and tons of love, despite the bickering of our three boys. But even their arguing has become an oddly comforting sound. When we are at home, we feel at home.

This idea of feeling at home is something that the hospitality and retail industries have tried to replicate. Cracker Barrel's "Eat. Shop. Relax." and Olive Garden's "When You're Here, You're Family" are attempts to capture and sell the essence of the comfort we feel when we're home. They want you to feel that you're welcome just the way you are. No pretense, no judgment—you belong.

But what is home? Surely, a home isn't composed merely of walls, floors, doors, and ceilings because that's just a house. A home is something more organic. A home is something that grows over time and is cultivated by the people who live in it. Each member shapes the outcome—whether it will stay a house or become a home.

For Jenny and me, going home is a comforting thought. For you, that may not be the case.

When people hear the word *trauma*, more often than not they think of abuse. A large portion of our time at REBOOT has been spent helping people overcome experiences of physical, emotional, psychological, and sexual abuse. Let me tell you, the wounds of abuse don't heal easily. While the bruises may disappear, the invisible wounds remain. I've often found myself reflecting on why abuse is so difficult to overcome. I've prayed and thought about it for nearly a decade, and here's what I've come up with: abuse is so damaging because it takes away our home.

The word *home* implies emotional and physical safety. Home is a place that provides shelter from the storms of life. In it we find refuge, space to heal, and provisions for the journey ahead. But victims of abuse experience a hidden homelessness.[1] We wander the world looking for the safety, stability, and support that should be found at home and provided by the people who love us. When we are at home, we should feel . . . at home.

But in many cases, the people who should make our house a home make it a place of violence and secrecy. They inflict psychological abuse through manipulation and verbal assault. They wound and weaken us while distorting our thoughts until they gain influence over our actions. They emotionally torment us by rejecting, neglecting, and threatening to leave us. They hide behind religious language used to justify their abuse, and everyone thinks they are wonderful—except us. They hammer down our self-worth and use physical harm when necessary.

That home isn't home at all; it's hell.

With physical abuse, we don't feel at home in our own home.

With sexual abuse, we don't feel at home in our own body.

With psychological abuse, we don't feel at home in our own mind.

With spiritual abuse, we don't feel at home in our own soul.

Jenny and I hope that our children will always want to come back home when they are grown and have their own kids. But for many of you reading this book, the idea of going home strikes fear in your heart because home was the origin of abuse.

Of all the chapters in this book, this chapter was the most painful to write. I hate abuse. I hate the injustice of abuse, and I'm heartbroken by the wounds it causes. I know I'm not alone. I know you hate it too. So let's hate it together, but let's also heal from it together.

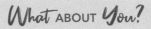

In what ways is your home safe and nurturing? In what ways could it be unstable or threatening? What was home like when you were a child?

Inventing Evil

Abuse goes by many names—domestic violence, child abuse, rape, spiritual abuse, and more. Each is a different form of abuse that wounds the mind, body, and soul.

These painful experiences are usually classified as either acute, chronic, or complex. As we haven't yet defined these terms, let me take a moment to clarify. *Acute* trauma results from a single dangerous or terrifying event. *Chronic* trauma results from repeated and prolonged exposure to highly stressful events. *Complex* trauma is the exposure to multiple traumatic events.

If you've been abused, it may be helpful during this section of the book to classify and categorize your abuse. For example, you might say, "I was *sexually abused* many times as a child." This experience was a repeated, *chronic* abuse. Or you might say, "I was *physically abused* by my spouse in an *acute*, one-time event last month." The goal here isn't to score or rate your level of trauma. However, as we've said before, we must identify what happened to us and, if appropriate, label it as traumatic. Remember that as long as our trauma goes unspecified or rebranded as something less detrimental, it will continue to have power in our lives. Calling it by an alternate, more forgiving name won't lessen its impact on our lives. If it was abuse, then it needs to be labeled as abuse.

But labeling it isn't always that easy because abuse comes in so many forms. We could write an entire book on the subject of abuse and still accidentally overlook ways you may have been harmed. During podcasts and interviews, people often ask me (Evan) how REBOOT has changed my life, and I usually tell them two things.

First, it has shown me the value of authentic friendship and brotherhood. I've never encountered a more loyal and committed group of friends than the ones I found in the REBOOT groups I have been a part of. Second, it has taught me to never underestimate the depravity of humankind.

There was a time when I was shocked by the baseness and wickedness of humanity. But now I'm not shocked or even dismayed—I'm angry. In Romans 1:29–31, Paul describes the evil acts people are capable of: "They have become filled with every kind of wickedness, evil, greed and depravity. They are full of envy, murder, strife, deceit and malice. They are gossips, slanderers, God-haters, insolent, arrogant and boastful; they invent ways of doing evil; they disobey their parents; they have no understanding, no fidelity, no love, no mercy."

I've come face-to-face with the truth that abusers "invent ways of doing evil." I've had to learn to guard my heart as I've listened to stories of the most abhorrent acts you can imagine. Every time I think I've heard the worst, I hear another story that hits me even harder. So as I said, I wouldn't attempt to capture in this book all the ways you may have been harmed because the list would be ever-evolving. Rather than try to address all the unique forms of abuse, I'd like to focus our efforts on how to heal from abuse, no matter the source or form.

What ABOUT *You?*

If you've experienced abuse, how would you classify it? Was it physical, psychological, sexual, or spiritual? Was it a one-time event or something that occurred often?

Forgiving with Boundaries

Excuses, excuses. Abusers are excusers.

Excuses are what I (Evan) often hear when I meet with someone who has abused another. It seems that there are always extenuating circumstances. They say things like "I switched medications," "It was an accident," or "It wasn't really abuse." On and on I listen as the abuser denies responsibility and allows the person they are abusing to defend them. Even thinking about it makes my blood boil.

Interestingly, I find that people of faith are often the most likely to justify and hastily forgive the behavior of their abusers. With the goal of practicing what they profess, they are quick to forgive and show grace without the expectation of change. The spiritual goal itself is commendable. However, while I believe wholeheartedly in the power of forgiveness, I also believe that actions should have consequences.

I was speaking at the graduation of an individual who had completed one of our courses when I realized I needed to further clarify something I had overlooked in our curriculum. A young woman in her twenties was sharing with the group how helpful the course had been for her. Part of the graduation process is to share a vision of how your life will look five years in the future. She began, "Five years from today, I will be married to my boyfriend and will be working as a dental hygienist."

So far, so good. She continued, "We will be trying for our first child, and I'll be actively involved in a great church."

Yes! Everything sounded great. "My boyfriend and I will have worked through his anger issues, and he will no longer want to hurt me. He'll know that I have forgiven him and will stand by him no matter what."

Wait . . . what? What was that again? Was I hearing her correctly?

Her five-year vision was to marry and have a child with a guy who was unrepentantly abusing her, *and* she was vowing to stand by his side no matter what—even if he kept hurting her. I resisted the urge to interrupt as she added one final nail to the coffin, saying, "And I just want to thank you, Evan and Jenny, for writing this curriculum. The forgiveness chapter was hard for me, but I realize that I need to forgive because Christ forgave me. Thank you for helping me see that."

Whoa. Somehow, she got the idea from our curriculum that forgiveness wipes away the consequences of abuse. This was either a serious oversight on our part or a gross misinterpretation on hers. Either way, immediately following the graduation, I flipped open the curriculum book, frantically examining each chapter to determine if I had been misunderstood or if I had inadvertently magnified the need for grace while minimizing the need for truth.

Unfortunately, that's exactly what I had done. But I won't make that mistake in this book. Forgiving abuse without first establishing immovable boundaries is naive and will likely result in further abuse. Forgiveness without boundaries goes by another name—enablement.

Forgiveness extended to an unremorseful abuser will usually be misinterpreted as permission to continue the abuse. We can't allow that to happen.

Perhaps that's where you find yourself today. Perhaps you've been showing grace to your abuser but haven't told them—or yourself—the truth. "The truth will set you free" (John 8:32) isn't a cliché. However, the truth comes at a cost. Most people, especially abusers, don't appreciate honesty. They are happy to accept the endless grace you extend as long as they are allowed to continue abusing you.

Should we forgive? Absolutely! Should we forgive without boundaries? Absolutely not. We'll show you how to do this in the next chapter.

What ABOUT You?

Has anyone ever taken advantage of your forgiveness? If so, how did that experience change your understanding of forgiveness?

Fighting for Your Younger Self

In 2017, REBOOT was given an award in recognition of our hard work and innovative approach. The guy introducing us said that we were giving people a second chance after trauma. In a grand fashion, he went on to share a few stories of people we had helped. But here's the thing: while his intentions were good, his description was wrong. The majority of those we've worked with over the last decade were abused as children. Before they could defend themselves, before they could speak on their own behalf, and before they could fight back, they were abused. We couldn't give them a second chance because they never had a first chance.

On average, more than five children die each day from child abuse.[2] One in four girls and one in twenty boys under the age of eighteen experience sexual abuse or assault.[3] A report of child abuse is made every seven seconds.[4] For these children, abuse entered their lives before they had the ability to set boundaries or stand up for themselves.

And here's the worst part: the leading perpetrators of child abuse are the parents. The very people who are supposed to provide safety and support are often the ones who cause the most harm. Rather than home being a place of comfort, for abused children, it becomes a place of fear. "When you're here, you're family" reads more like "When you're here, you wish you weren't." For them, home isn't where the heart is; it's where the hurt is.

I (Evan) have had hundreds of conversations with friends whose childhoods were marked by abuse, and I've found that the abuse was often normalized. They just assumed that their home was "normal." After all, they didn't know anything different. Sure, maybe they spent some time at a friend's house and recognized that the mom didn't seem angry all the time, or they told a friend about a relative touching them who didn't seem to understand what they meant. Those moments gave them a glimpse into a world where abuse wasn't normal so they may have sensed that something was wrong, but so what? What could they have done to change it? They were trapped. Their home was a prison, and their parent (or guardian) was the abusive warden. They didn't have any power. They didn't have any money. They didn't have a car. It was their word against their abuser's. Perhaps they tried to tell someone, but their pleas for help were dismissed as childish misinterpretations. Finally, one day they were old enough to do something about it, and they vowed to leave home and never come back. They ran, believing that distance and time would heal the wounds no one else seemed to notice.

But if my friends were sitting with you right now, they would tell you that while distance and time certainly helped, they didn't heal.

The anger, bitterness, rejection, and fear remained and for decades sabotaged any chance they had at healthy adult relationships. They would tell you about ongoing struggles with intimacy, emotional withdrawal, and distrust. Many of them escaped one abuser only to run right into the arms of another. A recent survey showed that more than half (51 percent) of adults who were abused as children experience domestic abuse in later life.[5]

The abuse switches hands, but it continues.

That doesn't have to be your story. You don't have to keep waiting to heal. Abuse of any kind isn't normal and it is never OK—even if the house you grew up in made it feel that way. You didn't deserve it then, and you don't deserve it now. You don't need to just "get over it" or "move on" as some may have advised. You need to heal by working through the abuse you experienced, and that process begins by making sure no further abuse is allowed into your life. If you're currently in an abusive relationship, you can get out. We've got some practical tips for how to do so later in the book.

If you've experienced childhood abuse, your younger self is waiting on your adult self to show up and fight for what's right. You are no longer powerless, under the thumb of an oppressive warden. You can fight back and peacefully defend yourself. You can protest the injustice of the abuse and give voice to its impact on your life. Tell your younger self that it wasn't your fault. Tell yourself that you have survived the worst and you will continue to make it through. Tell yourself that God has never abandoned you. He's been with you in every moment of pain and suffering, and he's with you now.

Fighting for your younger self may be in the form of mentoring a younger person who has recently suffered abuse. It may be volunteering at a local women's shelter or donating to help fund the adoption of children who have been placed in custody of the state. It may even be confronting your abuser and sharing with them the truth of how they hurt you. In whatever form it takes for you to fight, push back the darkness and invent ways of doing good rather than evil.

> Your younger self is *waiting* on your adult self to *show* up and *fight* for what's right.

What ABOUT *You?*

Looking back at your childhood, are there things you experienced that seemed normal at the time but that you now identify as harmful? Knowing what you know now, what would you like to say to your younger self?

Taking Back Control

As I said earlier in the chapter, traumatic experiences are as varied and unique as those who experience them. You may not have experienced childhood abuse. Perhaps you experienced domestic assault, intimate-partner violence, emotional abuse, spiritual abuse, or rape. Or you may have been the victim of a violent crime. While each is a completely unique experience, they all contain an element of psychological abuse. That's because all abuse is also psychological abuse.

The goal of abuse is to control and humiliate. Abusers distort facts and deploy every manipulative tool in the book to convince us that we are the problem, not them. They do the crimes and we do the time. We carry the guilt, shame, regret, and self-hatred they should be carrying. In many instances, the self-inflicted punishment that follows the experience may be as damaging as the traumatic event itself.

All abuse is also *psychological* abuse.

In cases where we are in relationship with the abuser, we may find ourselves trapped in an exhausting one-sided game of trying to keep them happy. Blinded by the fog of their deceit, we're unable to recognize the abuse while we're experiencing it. We cling to our abuser and forsake all else. And in the moment, we are certain that we're making the right decisions. But when we step back and the mental fog lifts, we begin to see how manipulative, harmful, and controlling our abuser has become.

A few years ago, Jenny and I were at a party with a close friend who we knew was in an abusive relationship. During the course of the night, my friend's boyfriend presented himself as charismatic, funny, and charming. Several people even commented on what a catch the guy was. We were trying to get her to escape the relationship, but each affirming comment led to even more confusion and cognitive dissonance. She thought, *Maybe everyone's right; maybe he's a great guy and I'm about to blow it.* Sadly, she stayed with him nine more months. One day she called us, and we met at a park near her house. His psychological and emotional abuse had turned physical. She had a black eye, a chipped tooth, and bruises on her neck and jaw. The spell was broken, and she finally saw the abuse for what it was. Jenny and I just wish there had been an easier way.

If you are currently in a relationship with an abuser, I hope that the fog is beginning to lift and that your eyes are being opened to see their controlling behavior. Talk to someone outside the circle of your abuser's control and ask them for their honest feedback. Be vulnerable with them and describe what's happening to you. Ask for their help and continue seeking wise counsel. The more truth you hear, the easier it will be to recognize the lies.

To anyone who has experienced domestic or intimate-partner abuse, we advise you to establish firm boundaries and develop a plan to find safety. Think of it as your "abuse exit strategy."

Remember the young woman who took our forgiveness lesson a bit too far? She ended up filing a police report about her boyfriend's abuse. He was arrested and is awaiting a court date. His harmful actions should have consequences. She has learned how to stand up to his abuse. She now feels comfortable in her home, and she's starting to feel comfortable in her own body again. She's setting the tone for how her home will operate, showing a strength and resilience that will be passed on to her children someday.

And, God willing, those children will live a long, happy life in a loving home instead of an abusive house. I hope the same will be said of you and your children.

A final note: if you are currently experiencing abuse, it isn't something to be embarrassed about, and you don't have to go through it alone. If you are experiencing domestic abuse, please call 800-799-SAFE. If you are experiencing sexual abuse, please call 800-656-HOPE. If you are feeling suicidal, please call 800-273-8255.

If you aren't able to call these numbers or if you need more immediate assistance, please call 911 or go to your nearest emergency department. There's nothing more important than your safety.

Learn how physical, emotional, and spiritual abuse work and why they are so damaging.

What ABOUT *You?*

Are there signs of physical, psychological, sexual, or spiritual abuse in any of your current relationships? If so, reach out to someone who can help. Call one of the helplines above or a trusted friend, counselor, or pastor. You don't have to suffer alone.

PART 3

Your Healing

Reaping the Rewards of Forgiveness

There's No Freedom without Forgiveness

Previously, we discussed the story of Ricky Jackson, the eighteen-year-old who was wrongly convicted of killing Harold Franks. He served thirty-nine years in prison largely due to the supposed eyewitness testimony of a twelve-year-old paperboy who had been coerced into giving a false statement.

Upon his release, Jackson was asked what he would do with his newfound freedom. He replied, "I intend to live well. But it has nothing to do with whether I'm here in this nice house, or whether I'm homeless. It has to do with attitude. I've been given an opportunity, you understand? And I'm not going to waste it by holding grudges."[1]

This man had lost nearly four decades of his life—four decades!—but he was ready to move forward, not look backward.

When asked how he felt about the paperboy, Eddie Vernon, it was clear that Jackson forgave him, saying, "He was just this goofy little kid who told a whopper. . . . It wasn't only him that put us there. It was the lawyers, the police, the whole broken system. And there are a lot of innocent men out there who are never going to get justice. In that sense, I feel lucky."[2]

Lucky? He felt lucky?

Let that sink in. He had every right to be bitter and to rage against the system that falsely convicted him. But instead, he chose to forgive and press onward.

We can all learn an essential truth from Ricky Jackson: there's no real freedom without forgiveness.

No matter how badly we've been mistreated or abused, forgiveness sets us free. Ricky Jackson could have become bitter. He could have carried around a grudge in his heart until the day he died, and no one would have blamed him for it. But if he had chosen that path, he would have just ended up in a different kind of prison. While not behind physical bars, he would have found himself in a prison of emotional pain, and he would have missed out on the joy of freedom. And after all, what good is freedom if we can't experience the joy that comes with it?

> There's no real *freedom* without *forgiveness*.

True progress isn't possible if we merely exchange a physical prison for an emotional one.

Some of us may have removed ourselves from the traumatic environment, but mentally, emotionally, and spiritually, we're still there. While we may be free physically, our minds and emotions are still bound up. Our spirits are still shackled. We may not be under the direct manipulation or influence of our offenders, but they still control parts of our lives.

But that influence can end today. Together, we're going to learn how.

We see two major pitfalls when it comes to walking in the freedom of forgiveness:

1. Failure to receive, understand, and live out God's unconditional love, grace, and forgiveness.[3]
2. Failure to offer that unconditional love, grace, and forgiveness to other people.

It's not shocking to learn that recovery courses aren't filled with abusers. Those people don't go to the bookstore and buy books to help them heal from the abuse they've caused, and they certainly don't feel controlled by those they abuse. Instead, many abusers just go right on living their lives and hurting more people.

If we're being honest, we may want them to suffer as we have suffered or to at least acknowledge the pain they have caused us. But often, they don't care about or are unwilling to recognize the trauma they brought into our lives. They deny, blame, excuse, and reject the damaging impact their choices have had on us. So in an effort to dispense some level of justice, we refuse to forgive them. By withholding our forgiveness from those who have harmed us, we seek to cut off the relationship and bring their awareness to our pain. But more often than not, it doesn't work. Instead, their ignorance or dismissal of our need to heal just adds salt to our wounds.

And so we grow bitter or calloused. We try to move on and leave them in the rearview mirror. But when we least expect it, memories of them and the hurt they caused are triggered by some sight, sound, smell, or experience, and all our pain-filled emotions come flooding back. Remember how we said earlier that denial doesn't work in the long run? Somehow, even though it may have been years since they initially hurt us, they are hurting us again. And again. That's because withholding forgiveness doesn't hurt them. It hurts us. They don't change because of our unforgiveness. We do.

When we withhold forgiveness, *we* become angry, emotionally closed off, guarded, and bitter. So if for no other reason than self-preservation, forgiveness is the best option. Forgive for your own good. Choose to forgive for your own benefit, and whatever ramifications this has on the life of someone else is between them and God.

Does forgiveness come easily for you, or is it something you struggle with? How would you like to see yourself grow in the realm of forgiveness?

What Is Forgiveness, Really?

One of the most common reasons we don't forgive is that we don't really understand what forgiveness is or how it works. Most of us assume that if we forgive someone, they are off the hook for their actions. We may also think that we have to resume a relationship with them. But while God commands us to forgive others, he never tells us we have to trust those who've hurt us or submit ourselves to being hurt again. We've found that many people are actually willing and ready to forgive once they clarify what forgiveness is and what it is not. Here are some examples of common misunderstandings about forgiveness:

Forgiveness is NOT letting the offender off the hook. We can and should still hold others accountable for their actions or lack of actions. When the court system is operating as it should, we may get the satisfaction of seeing our abusers punished for their behaviors. But more often than not, it feels like those who hurt us get away with it. The lack of earthly justice can be extremely painful to abide. But as painful as it is, we must remember that judgment is God's and God's alone. God will bring perfect justice in his time, of this we can be certain.

Forgiveness is NOT letting abuse reoccur. Forgiving is not saying, "What you did was OK, so go ahead and walk all over me." We don't have to tolerate or open ourselves up to repeated harm.

Forgiveness is NOT manipulating the situation to avoid pain. We have to be careful not to simply cover our wounds. Forgiveness releases pain and frees us from focusing on the other person. Too often, when we're in the midst of the turmoil after a traumatic experience, we desperately look for a quick fix to make it all go away. Some of us want to hurry up and forgive superficially just so the pain will end.

Forgiveness is a process, NOT an event. We might be pressured into false forgiveness before we are ready. When we "forgive" because we feel obligated or so that others will still like us, accept us, or not think badly of us, it's not true forgiveness—it's a performance to avoid rejection. Give yourself time and permission to do it right. In my experience, forgiveness happens in layers. We may forgive one act, only to recognize a deeper underlying transgression that we must also work toward forgiving. For example, we may forgive the action but find it takes longer to forgive the words that were said or how they made us feel. That's normal and it's OK.

Forgiveness does NOT start with feelings—it ends with them. While the end result of forgiveness is a feeling of closure and freedom, forgiveness usually starts with a mental decision. We lead with faith, support with facts, and end with feelings, not the other way around. If we wait until we *feel like* forgiving someone, we'll likely be waiting forever.

Explore what to do when the person who hurt us says they're sorry but that doesn't feel sufficient.

What ABOUT *You?*

Is there someone who hurt you whom you aren't ready to forgive? What, if anything, would help you feel ready to forgive them?

To You and through You

It's been said that forgiveness runs *to* you and then forgiveness runs *through* you. If it is true that "hurt people *hurt* people," then it stands to reason that forgiven people *forgive* people. But that's not always the case. If you are in Christ, you have been—and continue to be—forgiven. But are you a forgiving person?

We've all heard the term *grace* tossed around religious circles. *Grace* in a biblical context is God's undeserved favor on us. In other words, grace means we are given the gift of forgiveness even though we don't deserve it. But have we really let that sink in? Have we let it permeate our lifestyles? When we fail to fully accept and receive God's unconditional love, grace, and forgiveness, we lose our ability to extend that unconditional love, grace, and forgiveness to others. A vicious cycle is formed: as we fail to internalize God's unconditional forgiveness in our own lives, we open ourselves to unforgiveness toward others.

Breaking the influence our offenses have on us begins with forgiving for our own benefit and continues by accepting God's complete grace and forgiveness of our own failings. Maybe we feel like we didn't do a "good enough" job trying to heal. Or maybe there is a past shame or guilt that we've internalized. Whatever it is, it can be forgiven.

When we accept grace, we become gracious. When we accept mercy, we become merciful. When we accept forgiveness, we forgive.

> When we *accept* forgiveness, we *forgive*.

Let's take it even further. Forgiveness is not just a suggestion—it's a direct command from God. In Luke 6:37, Jesus says, "Forgive, and you will be forgiven." This isn't an easy teaching, especially for those who have been traumatized. Forgiveness is an act of the will. We choose to forgive as an act of obedience because God loves us and wants to set us free.

Remember, if you are a Christian, you forgive because Christ forgave you, not because you are seeking to earn a specific response from the person you are forgiving or from others in your life. We forgive as a witness to the rest of the world and as an act of obedience to God. Yes, I know it is hard, but God never said it would be easy. It wasn't easy for Christ as he faced death in order to offer us forgiveness. When we forgive, we are sharing in the suffering of Christ and being conformed to his likeness (Phil. 3:10).

Forgiveness is truly supernatural. By the world's standards, it doesn't make any sense. Our natural response is to say "screw you" and walk away. When we forgive, it can feel like a personal sacrifice. A sacrifice, by definition, is taking something of great value, something we hold dearly, and offering it to God. While it may be painful, this act of personal sacrifice is a profoundly beautiful act of worship. When we forgive, we are taking our offense, our trauma, our hurt, and our pain and laying them on the altar of God's perfect judgment and justice.

We sure hold on to our hurt tightly, don't we? Our friend and pastor Richard once said that unforgiveness is like hugging a cactus. The harder you hold on to it, the more it hurts and the more damage it causes—to you!

Maybe your hurt is unlike anyone else's hurt. Maybe you have been traumatized your entire life, and no one can understand the depth of your wounds. You've probably been told by friends to just let it go, but that seems like a dramatically oversimplified solution. After all, who are they? They don't know what you've been through! They don't know about the cactus you're squeezing! They've never hugged a cactus like this before!

Do you see how silly it sounds when you compare holding on to unforgiveness to squeezing a pain-causing cactus? The process of forgiveness isn't complicated. It may not be easy, but it is simple. And it starts with a decision. In order to experience the freedom that God has for you, you must make a decision to accept his offer of unconditional forgiveness and extend that forgiveness to others—even if they don't deserve it.

Imagine how good it would feel to let go of every piercing needle of hurt you've been clinging to. How much freer would you feel with the days of bitterness, resentment, hatred, and revenge behind you?

How might it benefit you right now to forgive someone who hurt you?

The Weight of Unforgiveness

When I (Evan) was fourteen, I attended my first summer camp. Evidently, no one could agree on a name for the camp so it was called the Northwest Ohio Valley Youth Christian Camp or NWOVYCC. For real, people referred to it as that all the time. I guess, in a weird way, being exposed to such a long acronym prepared me for my work with the military.

This camp had some amazing hiking trails, and like most Christian camps, the staff loved to leave campers with a powerful illustration at the end of the week to really drive home the point. So bright and early on our last day, the counselors gave us each a potato sack and divided us up into teams of eight. We began hiking, and when we came upon our first station, we saw a pile of rocks. Sitting on top of the pile was a sign that read, "Pick up a rock, write the name of someone you need to forgive on it, and put it in your bag. Pray and then keep walking." So I did. Of course, being a fourteen-year-old, I picked up the gnarliest, heaviest rock in the pile.

We continued walking and came to a second station. There was another pile of rocks and near the rocks another sign: "Pick up a rock, write something you need to forgive yourself for, and put it in your bag. Pray and then keep walking." I did as I was instructed, put the rock in my bag, and went on my way.

The hike continued this way for more than an hour. Every few minutes, we'd arrive at a station, follow the instructions, add a rock to our bag, and march on. After the fifth or sixth station, many of the kids were having trouble carrying their own bags. I was a big teenager, so I offered to help some of the younger ones carry their bags. But I have to admit that by station nine, I was wiped out. My legs hurt, the skin on my shoulder was rubbed raw by the string on the bags, and I was covered in sweat. As we approached the final station, a sign instructed us to go into the event center.

As I entered the large auditorium, I saw that all the chairs had been removed. The only remaining object was a cross, standing in the center of the room. These words were written on the cross: "Come to me, all you who are weary and burdened, and I will give you rest. Take my yoke upon you and learn from me, for I am gentle and humble in heart, and you will find rest for your souls. For my yoke is easy and my burden is light" (Matt. 11:28–30).

A camp worker invited us to lay our rocks one by one at the foot of the cross. After several others had gone, I stepped forward and knelt down by the cross. One by one, I pulled each stone out of my bag, read the words on it, and laid it down. After I had finished, I stood up with an empty bag in my hand, realizing that the burdens of unforgiveness I had been carrying—both visible and invisible—had been transferred onto Jesus. At that time in my life, this was perhaps the clearest picture of the gospel message I had ever experienced.

I'm not going to ask you to go on a hike and pick up rocks. You probably don't need a demonstration like this to know that the burdens you carry are indeed heavy.

Throughout our lives, we pick up pebbles, stones, and rocks. We carry offenses, wounds, bitterness, and even hatred in our hearts. Because we are adding only one rock at a time, we adjust and adapt to the added weight. But as life goes on, the weight of the rocks adds up, until eventually we're too weighed down to move forward.

The day I knelt at that cross and emptied my bag of rocks was the day that I learned the true meaning of forgiveness. It wasn't about feelings. It was about freedom. Some of us have been tricked into thinking we are free when in fact we have just grown accustomed to carrying around our hurts. Our minds and bodies have adjusted to the added weight, but that doesn't make our pain any less real.

You may feel like this right now. You're tired of the anger, the rage, and the pain. You may be realizing that you've been carrying around a giant bag of rocks for the better portion of your life. But there's someone who died to take it from you. Someone who died so that you could be free. You can start laying your burdens down right now.

When you set your offenders free through forgiveness, you set *yourself* free, and they no longer have influence over your life. As we close this chapter, I want to offer you the opportunity to experience the freedom of forgiveness right now.

What ABOUT *You?*

Forgiveness takes action. Merely thinking about forgiving someone is not the same as going through with the decision to forgive. It's likely you won't feel like forgiving someone who has hurt you. But you can make a choice to do so as you recognize that by forgiving others, you set yourself free. Here's your chance.

STEP 1: In the following space, write the names of the people you need to forgive. You may end up including your own name. It may not be easy, but it will be worth it! Follow each name with one or two bullet points describing the actions you need to forgive.

_____

_____

_____

_____

STEP 2: It is important to speak forgiveness out loud, not just silently to yourself. Here is a prayer you can use for this step. If you'd like, choose one of the names and actions you just wrote, then read the prayer aloud:

Lord, today I choose to forgive _____ _____ [name] for _____ _____ [action]. It isn't easy and it doesn't feel good, but I do it as an act of obedience to you and to honor how you forgave me.

STEP 3: You may want to repeat steps 1 and 2 several times. But it is also important to celebrate progress, so call a friend and share with them what you just did. Let them know that you're on a journey toward healing, and invite them to continue supporting you on it.

Knowing Who You Are and Becoming Who You Can Be

The One You Really Are

In 1972, Indian philosopher Sathya Sai Baba said, "You are not one person, but three, namely, the one you think you are, the one others think you are and the one you really are."[1]

All of your experiences—the things that happened to you, the words said about you by others, the things you've said to yourself—combine to shape your identity. They help define who you are as a person. But have you ever really asked yourself, "Who am I?" This existential question probably isn't something most of us have spent much time contemplating. But perhaps we should. Here's why: a person who doesn't know who they are will never become who they can be.

We aren't born with a high level of personal insight and self-reflection. We develop a sense of identity through our experiences. This is why trauma has such a powerful influence on our lives. Trauma disrupts our sense of self. Instead of helping us grow in confidence and obtain new skills, trauma causes us to question ourselves, live in a state of uncertainty, and adopt an identity that is a shadow of who we have the potential to become.

We also frame our identity through the eyes of others such as parents, caregivers, teachers, peers, and partners. These external influences have enormous impact on how we view our capabilities and the role we will play in the world around us. If those influences make us feel valued, important, and regarded, we will likely see ourselves as such. However, if any of those key influences are unpredictable, unreliable, or battling their own demons, we can't trust them to help us form an accurate view of who we really are. As a result, we will likely feel insecure, unimportant, and even unlovable.

> A person who doesn't know who they are will never become who they can be.

If your trauma occurred when you were a child, you may have felt like you had to fight for the love of your parents. You may have developed an "earner's mentality" that said you needed to act a certain way and then maybe, just maybe, you could earn the love and affection of those around you. If your trauma happened later in life, it likely had a profound impact on your identity as well. Where you used to see yourself as rational, self-sufficient, and strong, perhaps you now feel afraid, confused, powerless, or helpless.

Remember from our discussions about guilt, shame, and regret that our behavior is based on what we believe. Our beliefs about ourselves—which we reinforce with our own self-talk—don't just impact us psychologically. Our plans, activities, values, and ambitions are all shaped by what we believe. Following trauma, we'll often end up acting in a manner that flows out of our distorted identity. If we feel unworthy, we will act unworthy. If we feel unlovable, we'll search desperately for anyone to love us, usually in all the wrong places. If we feel devalued, we will sell ourselves short. These feelings are further supported by the shame that we feel. Recall that guilt says, "I did something bad," whereas shame says, "I am bad." And none of us are able to consistently behave in a manner that's incongruent with how we see ourselves. It simply takes too much energy to fake it.

So what we believe about ourselves, God, and others is actually really important. The question we must ask ourselves is Are our beliefs based on fact or fiction? As we've mentioned throughout this book, sometimes we need to look at our experiences with a fresh set of eyes. This applies first to how we see ourselves.

Right now, maybe you don't see yourself as capable, powerful, or purposeful. Maybe your sense of adventure has been replaced by fear or anxiety. Perhaps you feel like a shell of who you once were.

Well, here's the good news: while you can't erase the past, you can write the future. Yours is a story that is still being written. And our prayer is that during this part of the book, you'll reclaim or reinforce who you truly are. To clarify, we're not offering a self-help manual or motivational pep talk. We're inviting you on a path to discover not the one you think you are or the one others think you are but the one you *really* are.

What ABOUT You?

How has your identity shifted throughout your life? What events or people have shaped who you are?

Trauma Is Contagious

Trauma is contagious. It passes from person to person and generation to generation. Addiction, cycles of poverty, sexual abuse, racism, divorce, and domestic violence can all be handed down from one generation to the next. When parents don't heal from trauma, especially childhood trauma, their children are automatically at a higher risk of encountering their own adverse experiences. Compared with children whose parents had no adverse childhood experiences, children whose parents had at least one adverse childhood experience were 56 percent more likely to have emotional or mental health problems.[2]

> While you can't *erase* the past, you can *write* the future.

The potential downstream effects of trauma are numerous. Children exposed to abuse or household dysfunction are up to

- twelve times more likely to attempt suicide,
- seven times more likely to become an alcoholic, and
- five times more likely to use illicit drugs.[3]

We could go on with more statistics to show how homelessness, incarceration, illiteracy, and income inequality are directly correlated with trauma exposure. But here's the point: trauma is a gateway to many of the ailments that plague our society. Trauma spreads easily because it changes the way we view ourselves, thus changing the way we behave. But it goes even deeper than that. Revolutionary studies have now shown that our experiences in life actually change our epigenetic profile. In other words, on a genetic level, we internalize what happens to us.

Assuming you aren't a geneticist, *epigenetics* is the study of how certain genes are turned on or off based on our behaviors and environments. It is not a change in the sequence of our DNA but rather a change in the expression of our DNA. Scientists who study epigenetics have found that trauma experienced by parents can impact the DNA and behavior of their offspring for generations to come.[4] For example, our ancestors' experiences can change the way our bodies respond to stress today.

That means that our response to stress can be shaped and influenced by things that happened to our parents and to their parents and even to their parents. Stop and consider for a moment how this phenomenon may be observed in historically traumatized people groups. Could it be that the aftershocks of centuries-old unaddressed trauma are felt even today by people in communities around the world? If so, then imagine layering social injustice on top of historical and generational trauma.

I must admit that my (Jenny's) natural inclination is to believe that life is what we make it. But understanding the generational ramifications of trauma does shed some light on why some individuals and communities continue to struggle while others thrive. When the question is posed whether maladaptive behaviors are inherent or learned, we now know that the answer is both. Habits, beliefs, and cultural mindsets are passed down genetically and then reinforced through experience. We have to uncover these hidden mentalities in order to heal and put an end to destructive patterns in our own lives and in our communities.

What trauma did your parents or ancestors experience? How do you think their experiences shape how you respond to stress?

Writing Your Own Playbook

In addition to the innate strengths, vulnerabilities, and tendencies instilled in us by our DNA, we also possess a playbook for life that was handed down to us from the people who raised us. This playbook is our default reference guide for almost every aspect of our lives. It informs how we manage stress, respond to anger, handle our money, and even treat our bodies. Our playbook is an adapted and hopefully refined set of plays run by our parents or caregivers in response to their life experiences. And guess what, their playbook was based on their parents' playbook, which was based on their parents' playbook.

Plays for living are handed down from generation to generation. Some may be helpful, some are destructive, and others just need to be retired. You're in charge of which plays make it into your book of options and which plays actually get used. You are 100 percent in control of how you respond to what life throws at you. This gift is called free will.

Free will is quite literally the blessing to choose our own adventure. We have the ability to override our DNA-driven tendencies and to call our own plays. This divine gift gives us the ability to do what those before us did not. We can break generational patterns and take the first steps toward modifying the sequential DNA that will be passed down to our own descendants. Pretty cool, right?

But how do we do this? First, we remember who we are; then, we make choices to become who we want to be.

In a speech to the British parliament in 1948, Winston Churchill, paraphrasing Spanish philosopher George Santayanna, said, "Those who fail to learn from history are doomed to repeat it."[5] For healing to begin, we need honest acknowledgment of and investigation into the trauma that has been experienced by us and our ancestors. We cannot deny the cultural and personal ramifications that are, at least in part, a result of generational or institutional trauma. Denial won't drive us forward.

Living life in ignorance of our ancestors' traumas, victories, and defeats is like retaking a failed test without reviewing what we got wrong the first time. Sure, we have a playbook, but we've never studied it. We haven't discerned which plays handed down to us worked and put points on the board and which didn't. We haven't determined which plays can actually help us and empower us to help others and which are going to drive us into the ground. Please understand, though, that the point of studying our past is not to adopt a victim mindset or feel destined to repeat mistakes made by others. Rather, it is to learn how to build on that past to create a brighter future. The more we understand how we got here, the more we understand how we're going to move forward.

What ABOUT You?

Looking ahead, what "new plays" do you hope to design for your life that will break generational patterns of trauma?

Making Sense of Your Past

Knowing the facts about our past is one thing, but deriving meaning from them is another. It is the difference between knowing the elements of a story and grasping the meaning the story was crafted to convey. I could tell you the movie was about Rose De-Witt Bukater, Jack Dawson, a big ship, an iceberg, and a bunch of people drowning, but that isn't the story of *Titanic*. I'm afraid this is what many of us do when we try to understand our story. We read some facts and some dates and assume we know where we came from. But it isn't just the things that happened to us that define who we become—it's how much we've made sense of what happened to us. That's the goal here—to help you make sense of your past and uncover how it actually impacts you today.

Back in 2014, I (Evan) was working as the CEO of a fairly large technology company when, in less than thirty days, we lost several clients that accounted for more than 60 percent of our company's profit. Facing layoffs, pay cuts, and a PR challenge, I crumbled. I was paralyzed by fear, anxiety, and self-doubt. I felt ashamed, embarrassed, and miserable. I felt like I had let everyone down, and in some cases, they told me to my face that I had. The months that followed were among the darkest I've ever experienced. It got to the point when Jenny had to confront me because she was worried that I might harm myself. Now, mind you, this was happening at the same time that REBOOT, our little home-based nonprofit, was really taking off. So while by day I was falling apart, overwhelmed by depression and feelings of failure, at night I was seeing God move in people's lives like I had never dreamed. Jenny and I had money in the bank, and we had a nice home. When I would talk to others about how overwhelmed I was, they didn't get it. They'd say, "Evan, things aren't that bad, you're good," but it didn't feel that way.

I could tell that I wasn't responding well to the experience. I had just enough self-awareness and enough strong people in my community to help me see that something deeper was going on. My check-engine light was on and pointing me to examine the roots of these alarming feelings.

It just so happened that during this same time, we were hosting a weekend retreat for a bunch of families who had experienced trauma. The sessions were being led by our friend Leilani, and one of the topics was "Uncovering Limiting Beliefs." I was so busy that I didn't have time to review the content before the event began and I trusted Leilani, so I went in with about as much foreknowledge as the average participant. That weekend was a turning point for me because it taught me to view my past as the key to unlocking why I was responding the way I was in the present.

I found the sources of my responses. I learned that I had a deep-rooted fear of financial ruin, an unspoken sense of inadequacy, and a paranoia that everyone was always watching me. I learned why I didn't trust my decision-making skills. I found that I had an irrational fear of dying young or being stricken with a life-altering illness. I learned why I was always waiting for (or sometimes actually willing) something bad to happen. I didn't just uncover that these tendencies existed, but I also saw how they emerged from my unique story. I learned why I was the way I was.

And I felt so empowered! Just understanding the limiting beliefs I had adopted and how they influenced my current mindset removed so much of the anxiety and self-abuse I was enduring. I was able to take ownership of my feelings, and I slowly learned to manage them. The experience also gave me the courage to realize that I was living in conflict between what I was doing and what I wanted to be doing. I was the CEO of a tech company, but I wanted to be helping people overcome trauma full-time.

As I learned who I was, I was set free to become who I could be.

In October of that year, I announced I was leaving the tech company, and Jenny and I started REBOOT full-time the following May. As I write this chapter, I can't help but take stock of all the adventure and growth I've experienced because of that single exercise. It changed my life, and I want to give you the same opportunity. For me, the breakthrough was found in a simple activity that I have included here. For you, it may be found in combining this activity with a deep dive into your ancestry. I'm not sure. But I do know that uncovering the beliefs, mindsets, and habits that have been handed down to us is a tremendously beneficial and necessary step in overcoming trauma.

What ABOUT *You?*

Here's a list of limiting beliefs[6] that can deeply influence the way you see yourself. Read through the list of statements, and place a check mark by any statement you agree with or have believed about yourself.

This activity may look a bit overwhelming at first glance. Don't worry, it won't take more than ten to fifteen minutes. Don't overthink it. If something clicks with you, add a check mark. There will be a couple more steps to this activity, but just focus on this part for now.

LIMITING BELIEFS ABOUT MYSELF

What I'm Worth

☐ I'm only loved because of what I do for others.

☐ My feelings aren't worth sharing.

☐ No one values my opinion.

☐ I deserve to feel this bad.

☐ I must be perfect to be accepted.

☐ No matter how I try, I'm never enough.

☐ Everyone else is better than me.

Who I Am

☐ I'm screwed up. I can't be fixed.

☐ I shouldn't have been born.

- ☐ I'm no good. Everything I do is wrong.
- ☐ I'm a failure.
- ☐ I'll never fit in.
- ☐ I'm toxic to my relationships.

What I Can Do

- ☐ It's not worth trying because I'll fail anyway.
- ☐ I'm always a step behind.
- ☐ I'll never make something of myself.
- ☐ I'm not intelligent.

What's Ahead for Me

- ☐ My best days are behind me.
- ☐ I'm too set in my ways to change.
- ☐ I'll die at an early age.
- ☐ I'm incapable of change.
- ☐ I'll never get over this.

Who I Trust

- ☐ No one is trustworthy.
- ☐ Everyone will hurt me.
- ☐ People in power are always abusive.
- ☐ People will use what I share against me.

How I'm Accepted

- ☐ I can't be my true self.
- ☐ I have to put on a mask.
- ☐ People gossip about me.
- ☐ People pity me.
- ☐ People merely tolerate me.

How I Look

- ☐ No one will find me desirable.
- ☐ I can never lose weight.
- ☐ I'm not attractive.

How I Relate to Others

- ☐ No one wants me around.
- ☐ I don't belong.
- ☐ I drag everyone down.
- ☐ I should avoid making waves at any cost.
- ☐ I'll always be alone.
- ☐ I'm always to blame when things go wrong.

How I Feel Safe

- ☐ I can't let my guard down.
- ☐ No one really knows the real me.
- ☐ If I can't control everything, it's all going to fail.

How I'm Valued

☐ They all think they are better than me.

☐ I'm not reliable.

☐ I'm the last resort.

☐ No one wants to hear what I have to say.

How I'm Loved

☐ I have to do it all by myself.

☐ I am not loved by anyone.

☐ I'll never get married.

☐ I can't be happy unless I'm married.

☐ I can only receive love through sex.

How God Views Me

☐ God is never proud of me.

☐ God has forgotten about me.

☐ I'm a lost cause to God.

☐ God has let me down.

☐ God doesn't care.

☐ God doesn't listen to my prayers.

Whether you have believed any of these statements in the past, or you still believe them now, they're not true.

Not one of them is true.

What You're Really Worth

It happened a few years before I left the tech company. I had recently been promoted to CEO and was writing on a whiteboard in an open coworkspace when I heard a voice on the other side of the wall. The voice was that of an influential and successful business leader in town who was speaking to a guy who was, and continues to be, a friend of mine.

He asked my friend, "Have you heard how things are going over at Allen's company now that Evan has taken over as CEO?"

Not having much to share, my friend said, "Good, I think. Transitions always take time."

The business leader replied, "Well, I'm betting it won't be that way for long. From where I stand, it seems Evan fell pretty far from the tree when it comes to CEO material."

Yeah, that hurt. It is human nature to care what others think of us, and I have a lot of human nature!

I can easily slip into the habit of letting the approval of others become a driving force in my life. It is tempting to believe that I am who others think I am rather than who I actually am. It has taken me nearly forty years to learn that I can't find stability with a foundation that is constantly shifting due to public opinion. But in an age when information and opinions travel at the speed of the scroll, we are more susceptible to base our worth on others' approval than ever before. Rather than having a small group of people whose opinions we value, we have hundreds of "friends" on social media who influence our self-worth with each click (or lack thereof) of the "like" icon.

At the time, that person's opinion really mattered to me. I felt like I needed their approval. Why exactly, I'm not really sure. But I really wanted it!

Since primitive times, human beings have recognized our need for protection. By acting in a certain way socially, I increase or decrease the likelihood of my survival. If a pack of wolves were to attack my cave cul-de-sac, I want to ensure that my neighbors would have my back. Instinctively, this is why we care so much what others think. We know there is safety in numbers, and so we strive to fit in.

As I worked through the limiting beliefs activity, I had to discover a renewed source of identity ingredients. I could no longer draw on the opinion of others or even on my preset-DNA view of myself. I needed an external source. I needed a source that would tell me the truth about who I was and would point me toward who I could truly become. I'll get to that in a second.

> I can't find stability with a *foundation* that is constantly *shifting* due to public opinion.

But first, I have to tell you the part of the story that makes me sound super cool. Two years ago, I ran into that business leader at an event. He walked up to me with a big smile and shook my hand, totally unaware that I had overheard that conversation years before. We made a bit of small talk, and then I brought up the comment that was made. Of course, I was told I misunderstood, and he tried to backpedal. But I was feeling particularly froggy that day, so I made eye contact and said, "Hey, it's OK. Maybe you were right. Maybe I wasn't made to lead that kind of company. I don't know and I'm not mad at you. I'm actually thankful for your comments. Not only did they kick-start the greatest adventure of my life but they also taught me to never let someone who doesn't know my value tell me how much I'm worth."

Awesome, I know. It really happened just like that. But enough about me. I think you may need to take that advice to heart right now: never let someone who doesn't know your value tell you how much you're worth.

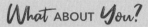

Do you know your worth? Sometimes we need to hear it from someone else to believe it. If you struggle in this area, here's something you can try. Select three friends who know you well and email them the following questions:

- What words would you use to describe me?
- What am I good at?
- What can you count on me for?
- What stays true about my character in good times and in bad?

You might be surprised by what they share. And if, in the future, feelings of unworthiness start to creep in again, you can return to these statements because you know they are true!

Replacing Limiting Beliefs

Nothing has ever been created without a creator. This book didn't write itself, print itself, and ship itself to your hands. Jenny and I intentionally made this book for a specific purpose and assigned a value to it. We designed it with a specific binding and paper type in order to withstand the abuse it would take getting tossed around in bags and cars. It was designed to be read, written in, and reread.

Likewise, you were purposefully created, and your Creator knows your worth. You were fearfully, wonderfully, and intentionally made. You were created with the potential to do something extraordinary in spite of your genetic code, the playbook you were handed, or the trauma you've personally experienced. The Creator gave you the material needed to withstand your trauma—even if it may not feel like it sometimes. The existential question Who am I? leads us to the one who created us, and the answer reveals a surprising genealogy:

> For those who are led by the Spirit of God are the children of God. The Spirit you received does not make you slaves, so that you live in fear again; rather, the Spirit you received brought about your adoption to sonship. And by him we cry, "Abba, Father." The Spirit himself testifies with our spirit that we are God's children. Now if we are children, then we are heirs—heirs of God and co-heirs with Christ, if indeed we share in his sufferings in order that we may also share in his glory. (Rom. 8:14–17)

Check that out! Through Jesus, God adopts you as his own child! The book of Romans describes how he "grafted" you into his family tree. First Peter refers to you as "chosen." Galatians says you were adopted and are now God's child and heir. The Israelites, or Jews as they are known today, have a dark history. Their ancestors spent generations living as slaves or refugees in exile after war tore apart their land. Whether they were subjugated by the Egyptians, Babylonians, Assyrians, or Romans, the Jewish people have experienced historical and institutional trauma both as individuals and as a collective people group.

Adoption was not common in the ancient Jewish world. For Jews, a person's standing was based solely on their birth. If you were born with it (property, position), you got it; if you weren't, you were stuck. Adoption was far more common among the Romans, who ruled over the Jews during this time period. For Romans, wealth had to be passed down within the family line. So if a father had no son or no child capable of managing his wealth, he would adopt someone who was a worthy heir. These adoptions were rarely of infants as we may think of adoption today. Older children and adults were usually adopted and would take over the responsibilities of managing the affairs of the family. Once the adoption was approved, the adoptee would instantly have all their debts canceled, and they would be given a new name—the name of the family adopting them. They would no longer be viewed as adopted but would be entitled to all of the benefits of a full-blood heir.

Here's the most incredible part: adoption was irreversible by law! As they were grafted into this new family line, a new branch of the tree formed. And this new societal position was transferable and passed down to their children and their children's children.

But what does this mean for us? A Roman was adopted based on their worthiness; we are adopted based on Christ's worthiness. When we come to faith, our past debts and sins are canceled, and we're given a new name. We are "born again," and with this new birth comes a supernatural spirit that allows us to live as we could not live with our natural DNA. We are no longer conformed to the patterns of this world but are transformed as our minds are renewed (Rom. 12:2). In Jesus, we have a perfect playbook, a flawless example to follow. And this blessing is generational. This blessing is contagious. It spreads.

Our adoption by God changes our story—not by erasing our past but by redeeming it. It tells us the true story of who we are.

Where there is fatherlessness, God is Father. Where there is rejection, God accepts. Where there is abuse, God restores. Just listen to what God says to you:

You may not know me, but I know everything about you.
Psalm 139:1

I know when you sit down and when you rise up. Psalm 139:2

I am familiar with all your ways. Psalm 139:3

Even the very hairs on your head are numbered. Matthew 10:30

For you were made in my image. Genesis 1:27

In me you live and move and have your being. Acts 17:28

For you are my offspring. Acts 17:28

I knew you even before you were conceived. Jeremiah 1:5

I chose you when I planned creation. Ephesians 1:11–12

You were not a mistake, for all your days are written in my book. Psalm 139:15–16

I determined the exact time of your birth and where you would live. Acts 17:26

You are fearfully and wonderfully made. Psalm 139:14

I knit you together in your mother's womb. Psalm 139:13

And brought you forth on the day you were born. Psalm 71:6

I have been misrepresented by those who don't know me. John 8:41–44

I am not distant and angry, but am the complete expression of love. 1 John 4:16

And it is my desire to lavish my love on you. 1 John 3:1

Simply because you are my child and I am your Father. 1 John 3:1

I offer you more than your earthly father ever could. Matthew 7:11

For I am the perfect father. Matthew 5:48

Every good gift that you receive comes from my hand. James
1:17

For I am your provider and I meet all your needs. Matthew
6:31–33

My plan for your future has always been filled with hope.
Jeremiah 29:11

Because I love you with an everlasting love. Jeremiah 31:3

My thoughts toward you are countless as the sand on the seashore. Psalm 139:17–18

And I rejoice over you with singing. Zephaniah 3:17

I will never stop doing good to you. Jeremiah 32:40

For you are my treasured possession. Exodus 19:5

I desire to establish you with all my heart and all my soul.
Jeremiah 32:41

And I want to show you great and marvelous things. Jeremiah 33:3

If you seek me with all your heart, you will find me. Deuteronomy 4:29

Delight in me and I will give you the desires of your heart.
Psalm 37:4

For it is I who gave you those desires. Philippians 2:13

I am able to do more for you than you could possibly imagine. Ephesians 3:20

For I am your greatest encourager. 2 Thessalonians 2:16–17

I am also the Father who comforts you in all your troubles.
2 Corinthians 1:3–4

When you are brokenhearted, I am close to you. Psalm 34:18

As a shepherd carries a lamb, I have carried you close to my
heart. Isaiah 40:11

One day I will wipe away every tear from your eyes. Revelation 21:3–4

And I'll take away all the pain you have suffered on this earth.
Revelation 21:3–4

I am your Father, and I love you even as I love my son, Jesus.
John 17:23

For in Jesus, my love for you is revealed. John 17:26

He is the exact representation of my being. Hebrews 1:3

He came to demonstrate that I am for you, not against you.
Romans 8:31

And to tell you that I am not counting your sins. 2 Corinthians 5:18–19

Jesus died so that you and I could be reconciled. 2 Corinthians 5:18–19

His death was the ultimate expression of my love for you.
1 John 4:10

I gave up everything I loved that I might gain your love. Romans 8:32

If you receive the gift of my son Jesus, you receive me. 1 John 2:23

And nothing will ever separate you from my love again. Romans 8:38–39

Come home and I'll throw the biggest party heaven has ever seen. Luke 15:7

I have always been Father, and will always be Father. Ephesians 3:14–15

My question is . . . Will you be my child? John 1:12–13

I am waiting for you. Luke 15:11–32[7]

God is speaking to you! You're the one! You're the one whose body was carefully crafted in the womb. You're the one he loves with an everlasting love. You are uniquely designed and for a unique purpose. You are not what others think of you or what you think of yourself. You are not what happened to you or to your ancestors. You are who God says you are. Period. End of story.

It's one thing to understand it cognitively, but we have to search our hearts and examine our pasts to truly embrace the identity God has given us.

What ABOUT *You?*

Take a look at the boxes you checked in the list of limiting beliefs and answer the following four questions. It took me some time and solitude to jog my memories of these events. But it was so important to identify the sources of my limiting beliefs. If you have trouble, ask God to help you remember. Don't skip this part.

- When was the first time I believed this about myself?
- What experience or person made me feel this way?
- How long have I believed this lie?
- Why did it impact me so deeply?

It may have been one single event or a long series of experiences that tripped you up. Satan uses both "microwave" and "slow cooker" lies to ensnare us in his traps. But these lies cannot stand when confronted by the truth.

In order for these lies to grip us so tightly, we had to have agreed with them at some point. We progress from hearing the lies to repeating them to actually internalizing them as our own beliefs. But Proverbs 18:21 says, "Words kill, words give life; they're either poison or fruit—you choose" (MSG).

We can break the power of these words and false beliefs by acknowledging them as lies and by following the next two steps:

STEP 1: *Break with harmful internalized thought processes (critical, hostile attitudes toward self and others).* Some of these gut reactions or behaviors may have been passed down by those who raised you. You may feel a defensiveness arise as you walk through these steps. Agree now to let go of those contentious patterns. We invite you to use the following prayer and fill in the blanks as they apply to your life.

> *Lord, I confess today that when* _____ [event] *happened, I was deceived and wounded and did not know enough to allow you to heal and protect my heart. I confess now that when this happened, I believed* _____ [lie], *but today, I call it a lie and ask for your freedom in this area. I ask for your help today as I confess my reliance on you for healing.*

STEP 2: *Replace the lies with truth.* "You will know the truth, and the truth will set you free" (John 8:32) isn't just an idea—it is a fact. Since early childhood, we've known that telling a lie can only result in having to tell more lies. Therefore, we break free from our identity traps by telling the truth.

Look back in this chapter at the list of things God says to you. Do any of these truths contradict the lies you have believed? Select one or more of the truth statements that apply to your own situation, and using the guided prayer that follows, fill in the blanks.

> *Lord, today I choose to agree with you and to believe* _____ [truth]. *I replace every lie and pattern of deception in this area with your truth. I thank you, God, for your love and care for me.*

Now we will combine the prayers from both steps to help us break the harmful thought processes and replace them with God's truth.

*Lord, I confess today that when _____
[event] happened, I was deceived and wounded and
did not know enough to allow you to heal and protect
my heart. I confess now that when this happened, I
believed _____ [lie], but today, I call it
a lie and ask for your freedom in this area. I ask for
your help today as I confess my reliance on you for
healing. I choose to agree with you and to believe
_____ [truth]. I replace every lie and pat-
tern of deception in this area with your truth. I thank
you, God, for your love and care for me.*

What did you learn about yourself through this activity?

Converting Pain into Purpose

Recycling Painful Experiences

Wouldn't it be marvelous if every painful experience immediately bore the fruit of personal growth? How fantastic would it be to step back after a difficult season and say, "Wow! I am so grateful for that time of trial because I already see how it has made me a better, more complete version of myself!"

Wouldn't that be ideal? Isn't that what we all want—to find purpose and meaning in the pain we've endured?

Well, it is possible, but it won't happen by default. For most of us, the journey to discovering the purpose in our pain will be a long and winding road, rife with unanswered questions. Pain doesn't naturally decompose into purpose—it just piles up.

I (Jenny) am the queen of what I call the "trash-smash." This is the act of smashing the trash down farther into the can in order to make room for more trash. I will trash-smash two, three, even four times. It's my signature trick—the never-ending trash can. That's right. I am a trash smasher. I accept it. But for real, it gets worse. Because eventually, the lid won't shut and nasty bits of spoiled food, partially empty Starbucks cups, and paper towels soaked in God knows what begin spilling onto the floor. Most people would probably just take the trash out already.

But I don't have time right now. I just smash it and vow to deal with it later. Not now. But later.

Maybe that's how you've been treating your trauma. Maybe you just keep pushing it down and pushing it down until you simply can't hold any more pain. The can is full, and there's nowhere else to hide it. It's not decomposing; it's just piling up. And now the trash from your past is spilling into other areas. It's sabotaging your relationships, lowering your quality of life, and forcing you to deal with it—not later, but now.

> Pain doesn't naturally *decompose* into purpose—it just *piles* up.

And trauma sure does produce a lot of trash: low self-esteem, shame, bitterness, broken relationships, addiction, and suicidal thoughts, just to name a few. This kind of undisposed trash from trauma infects our environment and makes us sick. It pollutes our entire existence. Everything smells like trash. Even our good days are defiled by its presence. And to make matters worse, Satan loves to add more trash to the pile. On top of the terrible things we've experienced, he offers us a special delivery of lies and self-destruct buttons disguised as painkillers to make healing even harder.

Trash is unwanted and unusable. It's what's left over after the usable parts have been used. What remains is worthless and can no longer serve a purpose. It's simply trash.

If left to natural processes, trauma serves no purpose either. It is harm caused for harm's sake. There is no redemption of those life experiences. In essence, we live through them and then live with them—end of story. But what if they could be recycled? What if we could separate the trash from the recyclable material? What if those terrible experiences could be converted into something useful?

Recycling is the process of converting waste into reusable stuff. In today's world, trash is being transformed into essentials we use every day like roads, soap, jackets, egg cartons, and even toothbrush handles. Recycling gives a second, third, and fourth life to materials that otherwise seem unusable. What appears as trash is transformed and given new purpose. And here's the coolest part: when I choose to recycle something, it doesn't benefit just me; it benefits everyone who will use the products that are ultimately produced. My milk jug becomes part of a playground enjoyed by hundreds of kids. My glass jelly jar becomes insulation that keeps people warm in an office somewhere.

One of the reasons so many of us have a difficult time dealing with our past is because we aren't able to differentiate between trash and recyclable material. I can promise you that God has an eye for recyclable material. He's like the original American Picker—finding treasure where others see trash. With God, recycling isn't limited to physical goods. I see it happening in the lives of friends, family, coworkers, and, hopefully soon, in yours.

Marie, who was abused from a young age, now mentors girls who have nowhere else to turn. Kenneth, who forgave his absentee father, now cares for him after he had a devastating stroke.

My sister-in-law, Tiffany, gave birth to a stillborn child. The pregnancy seemed to be going OK until she and my brother Ryan heard the words that no parent wants to hear: "We aren't finding a heartbeat." She was so far along that she chose to give birth to Elijah David Owens. He was so tiny. It was truly a heartbreaking experience. But the trauma didn't end with the birth. It continued with years of infertility and cycles of hope and disappointment with no answer to the "why" of loss and unfulfilled dreams.

It has been extremely hard on them, and I only know parts of the story. But they are finding recyclable material among the trash. Tiffany got involved with a group called Hannah's Prayer, an online community of mothers who have experienced similar losses and/or infertility struggles. She's recycling her pain into purpose and helping others heal.

These recycling stories aren't unattainable. They didn't require superhuman strength or skill. These are everyday people who, with God's help, are converting the waste of their experiences into something useful—something beautiful.

You can do the same. How could your pain be recycled into something good? Is it giving a voice to those who are currently afraid to speak out about the abuse they're enduring? Is it mentoring a child in the foster system who feels abandoned by their parents? Perhaps it's raising money for homeless shelters or volunteering to help someone find a job after a layoff. Maybe it's setting up a weekly meeting with someone who is going through a traumatic divorce.

I don't know where the recyclable materials are in your story, but they are there. Trauma doesn't naturally decompose into purpose—but with discipline, intentionality, and faith, we can find it together. There's a productive way to deal with trauma, a process in which pain gives way to purpose. We know it works because we've seen it time and time again. We call this process the Healing Equation.

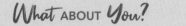

What ABOUT You?

What would it look like to recycle your trauma?

The Healing Equation

Here's the Healing Equation:

> First, we need to find *safety*.
> Second, as we start to feel safe, we need to seek out *stability*.
> Third, once we've found stability, we need *support*.

These three essential elements added together over time lead to healing. As a mathematical formula, it would appear as the following:

The Healing Equation

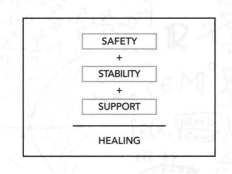

Throughout the remainder of this book, we'll use this Healing Equation to help you build on what you've learned and break the patterns of denying, crying, numbing, and running:

> Instead of denying, we'll acknowledge our trauma and take personal responsibility for our healing.
> Instead of crying, we'll grieve well, forgive ourselves and others, and let go of shame.
> Instead of numbing, we'll feel and heal the roots of our trauma.

Instead of running, we'll establish our identity in truth so that we can face whatever lies ahead.

Trauma healing begins when we find safety. Consequently, our initial focus will be on helping you find safety.

When we say the word *safety*, many things may come to mind. So let's make sure we are using the same definition before we go further.

Safety is about reliability and trust. When we're safe, we feel a sense of protection and security. We feel that things are going to be OK. Safe relationships are identified by grace and compassion. Since safety is the essential ingredient needed for healing, it must be present in order for any therapy or medical intervention to help. People who are safe don't live in fear. They don't wake up in the middle of the night with a sense of doom.

> Trauma *healing* begins when we find *safety.*

But maybe you do. Maybe you aren't feeling secure and optimistic right now. Instead of feeling at peace, you might have a never-ending alarm going off in your head, warning you that something bad is about to happen. If that's the case, it may be because you are trying to heal before you've established safety. Perhaps the following illustration will help explain further.

Let's say there's an earthquake, and we are all in a room together. What do you do? You try to find safety, right? You leave your belongings behind. There's no time for anything but finding a safe place.

Now imagine if I were to start assessing the damage in real time while the earthquake is happening. What would you think if I asked for some spackle so I could start filling cracks that were appearing in the drywall? Or if I started rearranging the furniture and straightening pictures that had shifted during the shaking? You'd think I had lost my mind, and rightfully so. That's because trying to fully assess or begin repairing the damage *during* an earthquake is a waste of effort. It is only after we have found safety and the earthquake has ended that we are able to deal with the aftermath. Only after the earthquake ends can we assess the damage, devise a plan, enlist the help of others, and begin rebuilding. But no sooner than that.

The same is true with the process we're talking about. Trying to deal with the damage caused by trauma before safety is established will lead to anxiety and frustration. And we certainly don't need more of that.

The question remains, Where can safety be found for the trauma survivor? Experts say that in the case of an earthquake, the best thing to do is to move under a strong shelter such as a sturdy desk or table. They say to push the shelter against a wall, tuck your head and neck firmly into your arms, and hold on to that shelter as long as necessary.

In the case of trauma, think of this strong shelter as God and the walls as a supportive community. God is the covering who's able to bear the weight of the world that is caving in around us. He's big enough to completely shelter us mentally, physically, emotionally, and spiritually.

God is as reliable a friend as you'll ever find. He is kind, loving, discerning, patient, present, and powerful. He's perfect. He won't leave you, lie to you, steal from you, or hurt you. He's a safe shelter. God is safe.

What ABOUT *You?*

What about the character of God lets you know that he's safe? If you are just getting to know him, do an internet search of "Bible verses about protection" and choose a few to write in your journal or in the margins of this book. Whenever you feel afraid, you can come back to these verses for encouragement.

Finding Safe Community

If God is the shelter, think of community as the walls in our earthquake illustration. Walls provide us something to lean against during an earthquake. They surround and protect us. A city with walls is a protected city—a safe city. Community provides the walls of mental, emotional, and spiritual support we need to heal. As we've mentioned before, one of the leading indicators of long-term mental health and resilience is the level at which someone is participating in loving, trusting relationships. In other words, you can't find safety alone.

Anyone who has been to war will tell you that you can make it through hell on earth if you have the right group of people around you while you're going through it. But let's be honest, safe people are hard to find—especially for trauma survivors. That's because trauma changes the way we view others. Trauma can make even the most loyal and optimistic person suspicious of those around them. But we assure you, they are out there, and here's what to look for in safe people.

Safe people don't lead with advice or recommendations on how you should be coping or healing—they lead with grace and compassion. They allow you to be vulnerable, and they are vulnerable with you in turn. They ask you how you are doing and stick around for the answer. They have nothing to gain from your friendship other than gaining a true friend. Safe people aren't necessarily counselors, pastors, or paid professionals—they can be normal, everyday people who love you and care about you.

When our bodies are in "earthquake" mode (remember the fight, flight, freeze response?), we aren't able to process everything that is happening to us. Safe people help us see from other vantage points outside our personal chaos. When our default trauma response tries to lead us toward making shortsighted life-changing decisions, a safe friend can step in and help us make a better choice. Safe people stick it out when others deny, cry, numb, and run.

What ABOUT You?

Take a moment and think about who would be a safe person in your life. One of the activities we give to many people we counsel is to build a personal List of Eight. This idea was given to us years ago by our good friend Bryan. He realized that many people don't have a list of people they can lean on when times get hard. He began challenging them to come up with a list of eight people they could call if they needed some help or encouragement. When we give this activity to people, it is very rare that they come up with eight names quickly. Truthfully, many people have a support person instead of a support system. They usually get to two or three names and then tell me they need more time to think. That's OK because two or three is a great start.

It bears repeating—you can't heal alone. No matter how good or helpful the words are in this book, you need others in your life. But be careful because sometimes we choose the wrong people as our support system. So here's the exact system we share with people to help them build their List of Eight.

BUILDING YOUR **LIST** OF **EIGHT**

My List of Eight

In the spaces below, write down the names of people you could add to your List of Eight. It may be helpful to reference the questions on the next page to ensure these are the right people to add your list.

_____   _____

_____   _____

_____   _____

_____   _____

"What makes for a good type of person to include in my list of safe people?"

Ask yourself the following questions as you consider whom to add to your list:

- How do you feel when you talk to this person?
- Do they take your feelings and needs into account?
- Is the advice they give based on your well-being?
- Do they tell you tough truths when you need to hear them?
- Do they celebrate your triumphs with you?
- Do they encourage you to be better than you were yesterday?
- Are they a Christian who lives a Christ-centered life?
- Do they have the capacity to give you some of their time?
- Have they experienced trauma or addiction?
- How would you rate the quality of their relationships? (spouse, children, friends)

Next, invite them to join your list. How can they provide the kind of safety and support you need if they aren't aware you need it? Simply send them this message via a text or email:

How to Invite Someone to Your List of Eight

"Dear ＿＿＿ , I am writing you to ask for your help. As you know, a while back I experienced ＿＿＿ , and it has been quite a process

210

to heal. I am becoming more and more aware of my need for a strong support system. I really value our relationship, and I trust you. I need honest, kind, and faithful people in my corner to help me get through this challenging time. I would ask that you commit to praying for me on a regular basis, checking in on me, and making sure I stay involved in a healthy community. Would you be willing to help?"

If you received a message like that from a friend, how would it make you feel? Exactly—honored (or a word close to that).

Then make an intentional choice to connect with them at least one time per month via phone, video chat, or in person. When you meet with them, talk about the real things in your life. Don't waste all your time on small talk. You can't change the weather and neither can they, but together, you can help change each other for the better.

Bouncing back from trauma isn't a seamless process. Earthquakes will come. There will be times when you won't feel safe, but don't give up and don't be afraid. You have the shelter of God above you and a strong community around you. That's huge! Take a moment to envision God covering you like a sturdy table and a crowd of people you trust surrounding you like a wall of protection. The safer you feel, the more progress you'll be able to make.

Was it difficult to come up with your List of Eight? No matter how many people you identified, be sure to reach out to them and invite them with you on your healing journey. And keep in mind that as you continue to heal, the list of safe people in your corner will grow.

Finding Hope in Unexpected Places

Building Momentum

We've seen it hundreds of times. Someone completes one of our trauma healing courses and leaves on the mountaintop. But a few months later, life is harder than ever and they're back in one of our groups. Time and experience have taught us that mountaintop moments aren't sustainable. What is sustainable is consistent wise choices. The writer Seneca once said that "no one was ever wise by chance."[1] He was right.

Your actions and choices will determine the progress you'll make once you're done reading this book. As you turn the last page, everything after that is your responsibility. Not that you're in control of everything that will happen, but you are in control of how you'll respond to it.

Our mission is to help you harness the momentum you've gained from this book to recover and build toward a brighter future—one that is marked by *stability*.

Stable people can look toward the future. Unstable people are slaves to the present. Rather than dream, plan, and build, they survive. We can never plan for tomorrow if we are too busy surviving today.

Have you ever met someone who seems to live their life in a perpetual state of chaos? They're always running late to appointments and appear to hop from one emergency situation to another. That's no way to live. It breeds insecurity, instability, and even more chaos. And to make matters worse, it is downright exhausting! Imagine the amount of energy it takes to live every day in survival mode. But that's exactly how trauma can make us feel. And this sensation of moving from one crisis to the next will continue until stability is restored.

We can never *plan* for tomorrow if we are too busy *surviving* today.

Stability is a state of stillness and predictability that enables us to improve our lives. It eliminates or at least mitigates extreme highs and lows. It establishes normalcy and routine. An environment of stability gives us the time and space needed to find our purpose and try new things. It gives us the runway needed to stop surviving and start thriving.

But stability and trauma don't coexist. Trauma tends to dump the contents of our lives on the floor and then leave the room. It leaves life feeling chaotic, confusing, and fragile. Momentum is tough to come by. Progress is difficult to measure. It can seem that we take one step forward and two steps back. Just as we start to feel a sense of order, a memory, event, or symptom emerges to remind us of the mess yet to clean up.

Trauma was strategically designed to be messy so that it would be intimidating to address. Satan doesn't want us to make progress. He wants us to perpetually exist in "earthquake" mode. First Peter 5:8 says, "Be alert and of sober mind. Your enemy the devil prowls around like a roaring lion looking for someone to devour."

If you've ever seen one of those *National Geographic* TV specials, you know what the remains of an animal look like after a lion has finished its attack. There's not much left over. In his book, *The Combat Trauma Healing Manual*, our friend Chris Adsit writes, "Satan doesn't want to make you feel bad, bum you out or hurt your feelings. He wants to devour you!"[2] That's why the apostle Peter tells us to "be alert and of sober mind." Other translations use the words "well-balanced," "temperate," or "disciplined" to describe the state of mind we should have in order to regain stability following the earthquakes of life.

There is a proven way to find stability, and it boils down to two behaviors that we'll look at in the next lesson. Setbacks are going to happen, and all of us will experience suffering again in our lives. But setbacks don't have to kick us back into chaos.

What ABOUT You?

How has instability impacted your ability to heal from trauma?

Not Your Fault, but Your Responsibility

Two behaviors in particular can help us to become stable. First, find stability by making wise choices.

We're constantly amazed at how often we say we want to improve our situations and experience healing, yet we make choices that work against our stated goals. Imagine that you go to the doctor because of a cut and you get stitches. Over the days that follow, there are some activities you'll need to avoid. You'll avoid playing certain sports. You'll avoid getting the wound wet. You'll avoid putting unnecessary strain on the stitches because you know that if they tear out, the healing process has to start all over again.

Healing from trauma is similar. There are some behaviors you'll have to refrain from while you're healing. There may be places you shouldn't go, people you shouldn't see, or things you shouldn't do—because to do so would risk reopening wounds and inviting chaos back into your life. That's the opposite of what we want.

All of us have go-to behaviors, numbing agents, and people we run to when we feel stressed or overwhelmed. Unfortunately, many of the places we run to work against our goal of healing. What are your destructive tendencies and painkilling behaviors? Our guess is that you don't have to think too hard to identify some people, places, or activities that you know aren't good for you. Be "of sober mind" and take a hard look at your life by asking yourself a few tough questions:

- What are my "go-to painkiller" behaviors—my numbing agents?
- Where are places I go that I should avoid going to?
- Who do I continue to invite into my life even though they aren't helping me get where I know I need to be?

These questions are about prevention, and they require anticipatory awareness. When we know our vulnerabilities, we can defend against future attacks and temptations more successfully. Just as you wouldn't leave your door unlocked if a burglar was outside, don't leave your vulnerabilities exposed. Wise people win at life because they are honest with themselves and put systems in place to help them avoid destructive choices.

So be wise. Be alert! Don't be surprised if some old symptoms try to make you numb and run. Don't get caught off guard when that old temptation comes knocking at your door again. Don't be shocked when an old friend or family member starts to bring drama into your life. Find stability by making wise choices.

The trauma and crisis probably weren't your fault, but healing from them are your responsibility.

Second, find stability by taking personal responsibility for your life.

When you were a kid, did your parents tell you, "Only *you* can be responsible for your actions"? It's true—yet sometimes we forget.

In order to heal from trauma, we must acknowledge our own role in the healing process. We cannot blame our trauma for all the bad things in our lives. We must take ownership of our actions and, in some cases, change directions. Trauma may have opened the door to dangerous painkilling behaviors, but we play a vital role in closing it.

Stability is impossible to achieve without taking personal responsibility for it. The trauma and crisis probably weren't your fault, but healing from them are your responsibility.

There are aspects of healing that only we ourselves can do:

- Accepting loss and grieving is something only we can do. No one can do it for us.
- Forgiving our offenders is something only we can do. No one can do it for us.

- Taking responsibility for our actions is something only we can do. No one can do it for us

You may have been victimized by trauma, but you aren't a victim. Those with a victim mentality don't overcome trauma. It defeats them. Those who identify themselves as victims believe their feelings and circumstances are always the fault and responsibility of someone or something else. They see themselves as helpless with little or no control over their lives. They are always looking for someone to save them or rescue them from their difficult situations.

But here's the harsh truth: even if someone got you into the painful situation, they probably aren't going to get you out of it. That's your responsibility and yours alone, like it or not. If you wait on others to help you find stability, you'll be waiting forever. Find stability by taking personal responsibility for your life.

What ABOUT *You?*

Take a few moments to answer the questions from above: What are your "go-to painkiller" behaviors? Where are places you go that you should avoid going to? Who do you continue to invite into your life even though they aren't helping you get where you know you need to be?

The Path to Stability

Let's get really practical. What can you do to rapidly create stability over the next few months?

1. *Make stability a top priority.* Commit yourself to consistency. Build a routine. Doing so will take a conscious effort. Don't stress out if you have to break your routine occasionally, but establish it. Here are some sample stability-building behaviors you may want to try:

   • Go to bed and wake up at the same time every day.

   • Eat three regular meals per day.

   • Exercise at the same time during the week.

   • Practice daily gratitude.

   • Read your Bible every evening.

   Find what works for you. The human brain thrives on stability and routine. Feed your mind, body, and spirit daily by making routine a top priority.

2. *Live within your financial means.* Don't spend more money than you bring in. It's that simple. Cut expenses and start saving money until you have a cushion of savings again. Financial hardship wrecks stability faster than almost anything else. If you don't need it, don't buy it.

3. *Don't overreact.* Drama is not a characteristic that defines stable people. Drama will keep you busy but unproductive. Don't waste your time rehashing a negative incident that already happened. You'll complain, bum yourself out, and end up right where you started. Put that energy to better use by investing in your future. When you see something upsetting on social media or in the news or when someone offends you, pause and give it three to five days before you weigh in. In most cases, whatever it was that was upsetting will have passed by then.

4. *Find stable friends.* Hang out with people who are of sober mind and make good decisions. Their positive behavior will rub off on you. If you've chronically made bad choices, find a wise friend to act as an advisor. If you've had a series of failed relationships, ask others who have successful marriages to help you choose and be a better partner. It may very well prevent you from doing anything rash and potentially retraumatizing yourself.

5. *Limit or totally stop your use of substances.* Alcohol or other substances may cloud your thinking and lead you to make bad decisions. Ironically, the time when you feel like you might need a drink the most is probably when you shouldn't. If you struggle with addiction, seek help. Addiction makes stability impossible.

6. *Build a personal emergency plan.* There's a high likelihood that you'll experience some form of personal crisis or emergency in the future. It isn't a good idea to wait until the building is on fire to map out an escape. That's why we've provided you with the exact activity we use to begin establishing a personal emergency plan at the end of this lesson.

With safety established, your full-time focus should be cultivating stability. Stable people make plans and work toward completing those plans. They have healthy relationships that stand the test of time. They have hope that is built on mature faith and trust.

Doesn't that sound wonderful? Imagine how good it will feel to be out of "earthquake" mode. Picture having a foundation that's stable enough for you to start dreaming and hoping again. It is possible to move beyond the pain. But in order to do so, you must be honest with yourself and others about where you are and what you need to do. If there is a hidden addiction that has developed as a result of numbing, it's time to expose it and get treatment. If there are suicidal thoughts that have continued to crouch outside the door of your mind, now is the time to make a wise choice and share that struggle with someone who can help. If you've been putting off getting a counselor, now's the time.

Listen up—indecision crushes stability.

You've lived long enough to know that even at your best, you'll make some wrong decisions every now and then. You're human! But don't let a few wrong decisions cause you to lose your decision-making confidence. Making decisions to heal and to move forward isn't an exact science. Certainly, when you're in the safety-building stage, refraining from making decisions is fine since the earthquake is still happening. But during the stability-building phase, indecisiveness will kill momentum. You'll end up on pause, and remember, we don't live life on pause very well.

So, press Play. Dream some dreams. Make some plans. Build your brighter future.

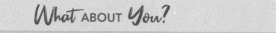

What ABOUT You?

What are three action steps you can commit to taking this week that will foster stability in your life?

EMERGENCY PLAN

An emergency is a situation that poses an immediate risk to health, life, property, or the environment in which we live. No one can be fully prepared for an emergency, but it's important to have an Emergency Plan in place that answers the following questions:

1. Where will I go if my home is not safe?
2. Whom should I call if I need to talk to someone?
3. Whom should I call if I am a risk to myself or others?
4. Have I saved a crisis line to my phone's contact list?
5. How much money do I need to have on hand for three months of living expenses?

Write your personal emergency plan and be prepared for future challenges.

Building a Support Structure

So what now? You're supposed to have read this book and be all better, right? Is that the idea? We are fully aware that, in all reality, this is just the beginning of your healing journey. It's a giant step in the right direction, but truly overcoming trauma requires more than just reading a book. Trauma healing isn't a linear process. You probably won't go from wounded to well in a perfectly straight line or on a predetermined timetable. Healing is always unpredictable. That's why we need support. Safety plus stability plus support over time equal healing.

On the days we aren't able to carry the weight of our past, supportive people and processes step in to bear some of the load. Support keeps us upright when the earthquakes of life try to knock us down. It steps in to offer correction, guidance, encouragement, and practical help when we can't tell which way is up. Support is the safety net needed for long-term resilience. There's a reason why support groups like AA and NA have been around for generations. Sometimes we just need someone to lock arms with us and keep us on our feet.

In California, there are these incredible sequoia redwood trees. They grow up to 350 feet high and weigh up to 500 tons! You'd think that something that huge must have an incredible root system going deep into the ground in order to stand that tall. But shockingly that's not the case. In fact, their roots are relatively shallow and go down only about six to twelve feet. With such a shallow root system, it's surprising that the trees don't fall over. Instead, these trees can withstand strong winds, earthquakes, fires, storms, and floods year after year due to their unique root system. Because the trees grow very close together, their roots become intertwined with one another, providing the support needed to stand for centuries. They literally hold each other up and share the nutrients needed to keep growing.

That's what we need. We need to interlock our lives with others so we can keep growing. Reading this book can't be the end of your journey or you may end up back where you began. Here are five optional next steps to take. Pick one (or more) and keep gaining momentum!

1. *Join or lead a REBOOT group.* If we've said it once, we've said it a hundred times. We can't be the best version of ourselves by ourselves. We need others in our corner. There is no better place to grow and heal alongside others who have shared similar experiences than in a REBOOT group. You can go online and get connected at rebootrecovery .com.

2. *Get clinical care.* This book and our groups are not replacements for clinical care. Clinical approaches can help you utilize additional coping strategies and/or medications that may benefit you greatly. If you've had a bad experience with a counselor, give it another shot with someone different. If you've never tried, consider it.

3. *Stay connected through MyREBOOT.* In chapter one, we placed a QR code for you to create a free MyREBOOT account. If you haven't logged in yet, now is a good time. Through this app, you'll gain access to hours of online courses, weekly challenges, and special events. This global community of overcomers will help you maintain momentum and keep a positive attitude. Also, this content explores areas of trauma healing we didn't have time to address in the book. So sign up and dive deeper.

4. *Join a church or small group.* Getting involved in a healthy local church will be a tremendous help in your healing journey. You'll grow your support system of safe people, and you'll learn how to tap into God's supernatural power. If you're not already involved in a church and don't know where to start your search, reach out to us; we'd be happy to help.

5. *Tackle other problem areas.* Trauma probably impacted areas of your life beyond your health. It may have affected your marriage, your finances, your family, or your faith. If there is an area of trouble or addiction that you need to deal with, let the momentum from this book propel you to seek further help. If the problem area is your marriage, sign up for a marriage counseling program or retreat. If it's addiction, seek treatment. Remember, stability and support will enable you to stack healing on top of healing to reach new heights. We've gathered some helpful resources that you may want to look into. You can find them in the QR code at the end of this lesson.

If none of those next steps jump out at you, that's OK. But do something! You need others. And guess what? Others need you too. Right now, there is someone who thinks they're all alone. They believe that they are the only one who has experienced what they've experienced and that no one else can understand. They are waiting on you.

Healing is meant to be shared with others. The healing you experience isn't just for you—it can also help lead others to discover their own healing. Maybe that means ordering a copy of this book for someone who needs it. However you do it, find a way to share what you've learned. We've found that many people grow stale in their healing journey because they have exhausted what they can learn through self-exploration. In other words, they've learned all they can by examining their own situations. Their healing journey is only able to progress further by learning from or helping others who have gone through similar hardships.

The first sign that someone is truly starting to heal is that they begin recognizing that others are hurting too. The second sign is that they feel empowered to do something about it.

When our lives intersect with the redemptive heart of God, we can't help but want to share it. When God makes beauty from the ashes of our lives, we become walking masterpieces that hurting people are drawn to. When God heals our wounds, our scars remain to tell the story of what he has done.

Someone out there is counting on your courage. They need to hear that there is purpose in pain and hope after trauma. They don't want to hear it from the experts, and they don't want to read it in a book. They want to hear it directly from someone who has walked through it. Your story has power. When you share it, you are looking the enemy in the eye and saying, "You didn't win. I'm still standing, and my best days are coming."

Ready to tackle other areas where you're stuck? Here's a list of helpful resources we recommend.

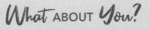

What ABOUT You?

Beyond identifying your List of Eight and making choices to build stability, what next steps do you see yourself taking to further your healing? Is there a church or small group you'd like to check out? Is there a course you'd like to take? Are you interested in counseling? Maybe you feel led to share your story. We invite you to take a few moments to ask God how he would like to use you and your story (even as it's still unfolding) to encourage others who are hurting. Does anyone in particular come to mind?

The Hope Factory

This is the end of the book. You've put in the time—the effort required to shine a spotlight on the dark places of your past, the courage to expose and care for your vulnerabilities, and the steadfastness to press on to the finish. But this is certainly not the end of your journey. You've got a lifetime of mountains and valleys ahead of you, and while you've got some new tools in your pack, there's one item of vital importance that we're certain you're going to need along the way. It's the one thing we wish we could magically give you when you close the back cover of this book. And that thing is hope—hope that your best days are ahead of you and that somehow, someway, this journey will be worth it.

You see, hope is among the most treasured and enduring gifts we can possibly possess. It's the key to resilience and joy and purpose and all the good things we want out of life. But as Evan and I have learned over the last decade, it is not something that we obtain (or retain) passively. Hope doesn't just fall into our laps, and just because we had it once doesn't mean we'll have it forever.

I believe everyone in the world is on a quest for hope, even if they don't know it. We are all searching for the things that make life worth living. The self-help and wellness industries alone are evidence of this. Many of us have bought into the mantras that tell us, "Life will be better if you have ____" and "You don't deserve to have to go through ____." But I'm afraid that in our efforts to avoid pain and "live our best lives," we're missing the mark.

Despite all our first-world comforts, ample medical and psychological resources, and unprecedented social connectedness, we're more hopeless than ever. In fact, the second leading cause of death among people ages fifteen to twenty-nine is suicide.[3] That tells me that wherever we're looking for hope, it's not there.

There is a hope deficit in people around the world, and it's because we believe that hope is found only in the absence of struggle. Well, guess what: the exact opposite is true.

You may have heard at one point or another that God's kingdom is upside down in nature. Remember what I said at the beginning of this book about God using the extras to play leading roles in his story? Well, that's just one example of how his behavior often seems unpredictable and backward to us. He doesn't operate as humans do. He uses the foolish to shame the wise. He makes a no-name shepherd into a king. He lets the last go first. He leaves the ninety-nine to save the one. He prays for his enemies. He turns the other cheek. He forgives seventy times seven times. He overcomes evil with good. He defeats death itself by submitting himself to death. And he births hope out of suffering. Romans 5:3–5 says, "We also glory in our sufferings, because we know that suffering produces perseverance; perseverance, character; and character, hope. And hope does not put us to shame, because God's love has been poured out into our hearts through the Holy Spirit, who has been given to us."

Check out the formula this passage gives us: suffering produces perseverance, perseverance produces character, and character produces hope. Of all the ways we'd expect hope to be produced, I'm betting suffering wouldn't have been at the top of the list. And yet, here we see that it is the unlikely place where hope, the rarest of treasures, is actually found.

For years, this was a mystery to me. I couldn't understand how painful experiences could possibly be the vehicles by which God delivers hope. But they are. Hope is the fruit of suffering.

Our friend Bryan knows what it's like to be hopeless. After a series of injuries and trauma left him in chronic pain and deep depression, Bryan swallowed two bottles of pills and laid down on his bed. Thinking that his suffering was finally over, he smiled for the first time in three years.

> Hope is the fruit of suffering.

A neighbor miraculously found Bryan, and his quick actions saved his life. This second chance gave Bryan the opportunity to experience a hope and peace he never knew existed and to be part of a story that is writing healing into the lives of thousands of hurting people around the world.

Not long after his suicide attempt, Bryan showed up to our REBOOT group. Having been raised in an atheistic home, he was not sure what to make of our words about God and faith. But he listened, and week after week we watched as he let his hard shell crumble away. We saw the breakthrough as Bryan began to feel his emotions rather than stuff them, to grieve his losses and put his guilt on trial. Bryan's eyes were opened to a whole new world filled with people who truly loved him and wouldn't hurt or abandon him. He met Jesus at a weekend retreat, and Evan and I watched in awe as the chains of guilt, shame, and regret fell off him.

We saw Bryan step onto the field of a new game with a new playbook, taking back his role as husband and father to his four children. Bryan became a passionate voice to others who were lost and hopeless, speaking on behalf of REBOOT and eventually taking over the leadership of the course location he initially attended. Bryan got a degree in social work and worked for our national headquarters to help with expansion and outreach for several years. He has personally led hundreds of people through our trauma healing courses, and he is living proof that God never wastes a wound.

I remember Bryan saying a few years ago that he was grateful for his worst moments because, in many ways, they radically changed his life for the better. Shockingly, it was in his darkest days, when it seemed all hope was lost, that God began his redemptive work in Bryan. The same can be true for you. Through suffering, you can embrace the profound and sustaining hope that can't be found anywhere else.

We all know there are no quick fixes to trauma. It's going to take patience and grit but do. not. give. up. James, Jesus's brother, writes, "Consider it pure joy, my brothers and sisters, whenever you face trials of many kinds, because you know that the testing of your faith produces perseverance. Let perseverance finish its work so that you may be mature and complete, not lacking anything" (James 1:2–4).

What does he mean by "let perseverance finish its work"? I'm inclined to believe that he meant something like this: Don't give up when you're already partway there. Don't let it all be for nothing. Yes, the pain is awful, but if you keep moving forward, it will mean something someday. And somehow, even though it doesn't make sense right now, this terrible experience will be recycled for something good.

Don't give up. Keep holding on to hope because God is faithful to provide it and because you are not alone in the struggle. Trauma may have been what brought you here, but soon enough, God's redemptive love for you will take you to places so rich with joy and purpose you can't even imagine them yet!

Love,
Evan and Jenny

Watch a collection of "Where Are They Now" stories from others who have finished the book.

What ABOUT You?

What do you hope for? What would make this painful journey worth it? Looking ahead, what in your life will help you hold on to hope?

Notes

Chapter 1 Restoring What Seems Broken beyond Repair

1. "How to Manage Trauma," National Council for Behavioral Health, accessed November 23, 2021, https://www.thenationalcouncil.org/wp-content/uploads/2013/05/Trauma-infographic.pdf?daf=375ateTbd56.

2. "Millions of Unchurched Adults Are Christians Hurt by Churches but Can Be Healed of the Pain," Barna Group, April 12, 2010, https://www.barna.com/research/millions-of-unchurched-adults-are-christians-hurt-by-churches-but-can-be-healed-of-the-pain/.

Chapter 3 Feeling It All without Falling Apart

1. Edward Tronick, "The Still Face Experiment," YouTube video, 8:33, posted by "Developmental Sciences at UMass Boston," March 12, 2010, https://youtu.be/vmE3NfB_HhE.

2. *How the Grinch Stole Christmas*, directed by Ron Howard (Universal City, CA: Universal Pictures, 2000).

3. Kibitzor, "How Much Would You Have to Cry to Die of Dehydration?" reddit, 2014, https://www.reddit.com/r/theydidthemath/comments/1y0n0k/request_how_much_would_you_have_to_cry_to_die_of/.compact.

4. Emily Roberts, "Why You Need to Release Your Emotions—For the Sake of Your Health," mbghealth, November 18, 2018, https://www.mindbodygreen.com/articles/suppressing-your-emotions-physical-health.

Chapter 4 Understanding the True Source of Your Trauma

1. J. Douglas Bremner, "Traumatic Stress: Effects on the Brain," *Dialogues in Clinical Neuroscience* 8, no. 4 (2006), https://www.ncbi.nlm.nih.gov/pmc/articles/PMC3181836/pdf/DialoguesClinNeurosci-8-445.pdf.

2. Kristin Lynch and Margie Lachman, "The Effects of Lifetime Trauma Exposure on Cognitive Functioning in Midlife," *Journal of Traumatic Stress* 33, no. 5 (2020): 773–82.

3. Erika Wolf and Paula Schnurr, "Posttraumatic Stress Disorder–Related Cardiovascular Disease and Accelerated Cellular Aging," *Psychiatric Annals* 46 (2016): 527–32.

4. Shira Maguen et al., "Association of Mental Health Problems with Gastrointestinal Disorders in Iraq and Afghanistan Veterans," *Depression and Anxiety* 31(2014): 160–65.

5. Huan Song et al., "Association of Stress-Related Disorders with Subsequent Autoimmune Disease," *JAMA* 319, no. 23 (2018): 2388–400.

Chapter 5 Loss

1. Chris Adsit, *The Combat Trauma Healing Manual* (Newport News, VA: Military Ministry Press, 2008), 66.

2. John W. James and Russell Friedman, *The Grief Recovery Handbook, 20th Anniversary Expanded Edition: The Action Program for Moving Beyond Death, Divorce, and Other Losses including Health, Career, and Faith* (New York: HarperCollins, 2017).

3. The term *Gold Star parent* refers to a mother or father who has lost a child in the line of duty of military service.

Chapter 6 Guilt, Shame, and Regret

1. Matthew Shaer, "After 39 Years of Wrongful Imprisonment, Ricky Jackson Is Finally Free," *Smithsonian*, January 2017, https://www.smithsonianmag.com/history/years-wrongful-imprisonment-ricky-jackson-finally-free-180961434/.

2. Brené Brown has said something similar in her TED Talk "Listening to Shame." You can access her talk at https://youtu.be/psN1DORYYV0.

3. Sissy Gavrilaki, Quote and Quote, April 4, 2016, https://www.quoteandquote.com/quote/?id=1665.

Chapter 8 Hurt and Abuse

1. T. Burke, "Housing and Poverty: Then and Now," in *Australian Poverty*, ed. Ruth Fincher and John Nieuwenhuysen (Melbourne: Melbourne University Press, 1998), 165–84.

2. "Child Maltreatment 2019," U.S. Department of Health & Human Services, Children's Bureau, 2019, publication date January 14, 2021, https://www.acf.hhs.gov/cb/report/child-maltreatment-2019.

3. David Finkelhor et al., "The Lifetime Prevalence of Child Sexual Abuse and Sexual Assault Assessed in Late Adolescence," *Journal of Adolescent Health* 55, no. 3 (September 2014): 329–33.

4. "Child Maltreatment 2019," U.S. Department of Health & Human Services.

5. "People Who Were Abused as Children Are More Likely to Be Abused as an Adult," Office for National Statistics, September 27, 2017, https://www.ons.gov.uk/peoplepopulationandcommunity/crimeandjustice/articles/peoplewhowereabusedaschildrenaremorelikelytobeabusedasanadult/2017-09-27.

Chapter 9 Reaping the Rewards of Forgiveness

1. Shaer, "After 39 Years of Wrongful Imprisonment."
2. Shaer, "After 39 Years of Wrongful Imprisonment."
3. David Seamands, *Healing for Damaged Emotions Workbook* (Colorado Springs: David C Cook, 2015), 45.

Chapter 10 Knowing Who You Are and Becoming Who You Can Be

1. Sathya Sai Baba, "'Kama' and 'Krodha,'" Sai Speaks, May 28, 1972, https://saispeaks.sathyasai.org/discourse/kama-and-krodha.
2. Adam Schickedanz et al., "Parents' Adverse Childhood Experiences and Their Children's Behavioral Health Problems," *Pediatrics* 142, no. 2 (August 2018), https://pediatrics.aappublications.org/content/pediatrics/142/2/e20180023.full.pdf.
3. Vincent J. Felitti et al., "Relationship of Childhood Abuse and Household Dysfunction to Many of the Leading Causes of Death in Adults: The Adverse Childhood Experiences (ACE) Study," *American Journal of Preventive Medicine* 14, no. 4 (May 1998): 245–58.
4. Amy Lehrner and Rachel Yehuda, "Cultural Trauma and Epigenetic Inheritance," *Development and Psychopathology* 30, no. 5 (December 2018): 1763–77.
5. Laurence Geller, "Churchill in the News," International Churchill Society, October 21, 2018, https://winstonchurchill.org/resources/in-the-media/churchill-in-the-news/folger-library-churchills-shakespeare/.
6. Terry Tuinder, "What Are Your Ungodly Beliefs?" Experiencing His Victory, https://www.experiencinghisvictory.com/what-are-your-ungodly-beliefs/#.
7. "Father's Love Letter: An Intimate Message from God to You," Father Heart Communications, 1999, www.FathersLoveLetter.com, used by permission.

Chapter 12 Finding Hope in Unexpected Places

1. Lucius Annaeus Seneca Quotes, BrainyQuote.com, accessed December 22, 2021, https://www.brainyquote.com/quotes/lucius_annaeus_seneca_108502.
2. Adsit, *Combat Trauma Healing Manual*, 15.
3. United Nations, "One Person Dies by Suicide Every 40 Seconds: New UN Health Agency Report," UN News, September 9, 2019, https://news.un.org/en/story/2019/09/1045892.

Evan Owens is the cofounder and executive director of REBOOT Recovery. Evan has authored several trauma healing course curriculum books and is the host of the *REBOOT Recovery Show* podcast. He is often featured as a keynote and panel presenter at conferences. Evan believes in empowering everyday people to help their friends and neighbors who are struggling in the wake of painful experiences. As such, Evan trains small group leaders, pastors, and everyday people around the world how to respond to those who are hurting. His unique blend of humor and inspiration enables people to absorb complex topics without feeling overwhelmed.

Jenny Owens, OTR/L, OTD, is the cofounder of REBOOT Recovery and an occupational therapist. She previously worked for the Department of Defense treating active-duty soldiers with traumatic brain injury and post-traumatic stress. Jenny has contributed to numerous occupational therapy publications, including the *Mild Traumatic Brain Injury Rehabilitation Toolkit* (2015), Traumatic Brain Injury: Interventions to Support Occupational Performance (2014), and *Occupational Therapy for Physical Dysfunction*, 7th ed. (2013). A strong believer in the power of relationships, Jenny believes that authentic community is key in helping people heal from painful experiences. She and Evan have three young children, and she enjoys having coffee with friends, cooking, and traveling.

Connect with
EVAN AND JENNY

Learn more about **REBOOT Recovery** and recovering from trauma by connecting with Evan and Jenny online.

 @RebootRecovery | @EvanandJennyOwens

 @RebootRecovery | @EvanandJennyOwens